P9-EEL-126

easy grilling

easy grilling

simple recipes for outdoor grills

RYLAND
PETERS
& SMALL

LONDON NEW YORK

Senior Designer Toni Kay
Editor Rebecca Woods
Picture Research Emily Westlake
Production Toby Marshall
Art Director Leslie Harrington
Publishing Director Alison Starling

Indexer Hilary Bird

First published in the USA in 2011
by Ryland Peters & Small Inc.,
519 Broadway, 5th Floor
New York, NY10012
www.rylandpeters.com

10 9 8 7 6 5 4 3 2 1

Text © Ghillie Başan, Fiona Beckett, Maxine
Clark, Ross Dobson, Jane Noraika, Louise
Pickford, Fiona Smith, Lindy Wildsmith, and
Ryland Peters & Small 2011

Design and commissioned photographs
© Ryland Peters & Small 2011

ISBN: 978-1-84975-111-7

A CIP record for this book has been applied for.

Printed and bound in China

contents

introduction

Outdoor grills are one of the best ways to make the most of a warm summer's day. Adaptable to any occasion—from an impromptu meal for two on a city balcony, to a large party in a country garden—grills are so versatile and always seem to inject a sense of adventure into cooking. Whether you choose a gas grill, for the convenience of being able to spark up as soon as the clouds part, or are wedded to the delicious smoky taste achieved when cooking over coals, grilling has become one of our favorite methods of cooking and entertaining.

In celebration of outdoor cooking, *Easy Grilling* is full of recipes which are simple to prepare, often in advance, so that you can relax and enjoy the al fresco setting and the company. Along with classics, such as cheeseburgers and chicken wings, are recipes inspired from around the world. From Chicken Kabobs Moroccan-style, to Vietnamese Pork Balls, Sicilian-spiced Sea Bass to Mexican-style Cornish Hens, there is something here to excite every taste bud. But if those don't tempt, turn straight to the Sauces, Marinades, & Dips chapter and create your own flavor sensations.

What many people don't realize is that grills are not only for your burgers and sausages. Vegetables are also delicious when prepared over coals and so *Easy Grilling* includes lots of great ideas for exciting vegetable sides and original vegetarian options. With suggestions for grilled desserts and delicious drinks too, this collection of recipes will inspire you to create a mouthwatering grilled feast, full of the aromas of summer.

grilling basics

While cooking on a outdoor grill is much simpler than you may imagine, there are a few things to remember before you start cooking. Follow the guidelines below for handy hints on choosing and making the most of your grill, and essential tips on fire and food safety, to keep everyone safe and happy.

Choosing a grill

Outdoor grills come in all shapes, sizes, varieties, and prices—from the small disposable aluminum ones sold in supermarkets or hardware stores, to the larger and often hugely expensive covered grills. Some grills have both a grill rack and a flat plate offering versatility, but this is not essential. The recipes will work on any of the following.

Purists would probably argue for charcoal to fuel their grills, but many people prefer and find it easier to opt for gas or electric ones. It is certainly debatable as to what will give the best flavor to the food, but it comes down to personal choice.

For a charcoal grill, you can use either standard briquettes or opt for hardwood lump charcoal. The former may contain chemicals from the process used to make it, which although totally safe may effect the flavor of the food cooked over it. Hardwood lump charcoal is not as readily available as the briquettes but contains no additives, burns easily,

gets far hotter, and lasts longer.

Portable grills are essential if you want to cook away from home (unless your chosen site has permanent grills) and these too come in a wide selection of styles. Again be aware of weight, the lighter the better, someone has to carry it. Portable grills can be either charcoal or gas, but remember coals stay hot for sometime so you must find somewhere you can legally and safely leave them or wait until they are completely cool before packing them in a bag to take with you.

Safety is extremely important in grilling, especially if you are in parkland as many places will be a fire risk. Be sensible and set the grill up away from dry timber or grass and always take a fire blanket or, if possible, a small portable fire extinguisher with you.

Cooking on a charcoal grill

Arrange the fuel in as large an area as your grill will allow, at least 4 inches deep and leaving a little

room around the edges. Place a few fire lighters in amongst the coals and light these using a taper or matches—these will help to get the fire started. Once the coals are burning, leave for about 40–45 minutes until all the flames have subsided and the coals are covered in grey ash. Hold your hand about 5 inches above the fire and count how long it can stay there. A hot fire will be only a couple of seconds a medium hot fire three to four seconds and a cool fire five to six seconds.

You can also determine the temperature for cooking by the height of the grill over the coals. Most charcoal grills have several rungs to set the wire rack on, the closest to the heat being the hottest and the furthest away, the coolest.

Cleaning is best done after you have finished cooking but whilst the grill is still assembled so that any residual bits of food stuck to the grill can be brushed off into the fire. Do not clean the grill rack with soap

or water, just scrub well with a wire brush (see equipment below).

Cooking on a gas or electric grill

Gas and electric grills can be adjusted in the same way as a domestic stove, by turning the temperature up or down. They often come with a hood enabling you to cover the food as it grills, which produces a similar effect to roasting. Alternatively, leave the lid off and grill as normal.

It is important to preheat a gas or electric grill until it is really hot before adding the food and then reduce the heat as necessary. This will enable the food to brown quickly on the outside sealing in the flavor in the same way as a more traditional charcoal grill will.

Cleaning is also done in the same way as for the charcoal grill, although you can buy special cleaners from hardware stores. For best results, follow the instructions on the back of individual products.

Equipment

Long handled tongs are essential so that you can easily turn over any foods you are cooking without allowing your hands to get too close to the heat where they can get scorched. Do not leave the tongs on or near the heat as they too can get very hot.

Skewers can be either bamboo or metal. Bamboo skewers are disposable and will need to be pre-soaked before use, which prevents them from burning over a high heat. Metal skewers are readily available from hardware stores but remember they can get very hot, so turn them using either a dish towel or the tongs.

A sturdy wire brush is the best method for cleaning and removing bits of stuck-on foods from the surface of the grill or flat plate. Give the grill a good scrub all over each time you have finished cooking and rub the flat plate with a little oil to season it each time.

Food preparation and safety

Get all the preparation done in advance—the day, the morning, or an hour or two before you eat. Marinating times in the recipes are flexible, so do what suits you. Salsas, relishes, dressings, and salads can be made in advance, but green salads should be dressed at the last minute. Once prepared, cover the food and refrigerate or store it in a cool place until you are ready to cook or serve it.

Most of the foods cooked on the grill will have started off raw. Although they must be stored in the refrigerator, it is best to return them to room temperature for about an hour before cooking. Always keep food covered with plastic wrap or a clean dish towel while they are waiting to be cooked to keep off the bugs. Once it has reached room temperature, food should be cooked as quickly as possible to prevent it from spoiling.

Once the coals are ready, arrange the meat on the grill and give it time to brown before turning. Once the meat has browned, turn it frequently and move it around the grill to ensure even cooking. You may need to raise the grill height if the cooking is too fast, or lower it so that it is nearer the coals if it is too slow. To lower the heat, dampen the coals slightly or close the air vent.

Make sure you cook chicken, burgers, and pork thoroughly. They should be piping hot all the way through, none of the meat should be pink, and the juices should run clear. Cut into meat to make sure it is cooked thoroughly. One of the major causes of food poisoning is cross contamination, so it is essential to keep raw and cooked food apart. When transferring cooked meats, fish, or poultry from the grill, make sure to use clean utensils and place them on a clean cutting board or platter, not back in the unwashed dish you used to transport them to the grill.

sauces, marinades,
& dips

Thai spice marinade

2 lemongrass stalks

6 kaffir lime leaves

2 garlic cloves, coarsely chopped

1-inch piece fresh ginger, peeled and coarsely chopped

4 cilantro roots, washed and dried

2 small fresh red bird's eye chiles, seeded and coarsely chopped

1 cup extra virgin olive oil

2 tablespoons sesame oil

2 tablespoons Thai fish sauce

MAKES ABOUT 1½ CUPS

Using a sharp knife, trim the lemongrass stalks to 6 inches, then remove and discard the tough outer layers. Chop the inner stalk coarsely.

Put the lemongrass, lime leaves, garlic, ginger, cilantro, and chiles into a mortar and pound with a pestle to release the aromas.

Put the mixture into a bowl, add the oils and fish sauce, and set aside to infuse until ready to use.

minted yogurt marinade

2 teaspoons coriander seeds

1 teaspoon cumin seeds

1 cup thick yogurt

freshly squeezed juice of ½ lemon

1 tablespoon extra virgin olive oil

2 garlic cloves, crushed

1 teaspoon grated fresh ginger

½ teaspoon sea salt

2 tablespoons chopped fresh mint

¼ teaspoon ground chiles

MAKES ABOUT 1¼ CUPS

Put the coriander and cumin seeds into a dry skillet and toast over medium heat until golden and aromatic. Remove from the heat and let cool. Transfer to a spice grinder (or clean coffee grinder) and crush to a coarse powder. Alternatively, use a mortar and pestle.

Put the spices into a bowl, add the yogurt, lemon juice, olive oil, garlic, ginger, salt, mint, and ground chiles and mix well. Set aside to infuse until ready to use.

herb, lemon, and garlic marinade

2 sprigs of fresh rosemary

2 sprigs of fresh thyme

pared zest of 1 unwaxed lemon

4 bay leaves

2 garlic cloves, coarsely chopped

1 teaspoon black peppercorns, coarsely crushed

1 cup extra virgin olive oil

MAKES ABOUT 1½ CUPS

Strip the rosemary and thyme leaves from the stalks and put into a mortar. Add the lemon zest, bay leaves, and garlic and pound with a pestle to release the aromas.

Put the mixture into a bowl and add the crushed peppercorns and olive oil. Set aside to infuse until ready to use.

Creole rub

½ small onion, finely chopped

1 garlic clove, finely chopped

1 tablespoon chopped fresh thyme

1 tablespoon paprika

1 teaspoon ground cumin

¼ teaspoon cayenne pepper

1 tablespoon brown sugar

1 teaspoon sea salt

a little freshly ground black pepper

MAKES ABOUT 6 TABLESPOONS

Put all the ingredients into a small bowl, stir well, and set aside to infuse until ready to use.

Moroccan rub

1 tablespoon coriander seeds

1 teaspoon cumin seeds

2 cinnamon sticks

1 teaspoon whole allspice berries

6 cloves

a pinch of saffron threads

1 teaspoon ground turmeric

2 teaspoons dried onion flakes

½ teaspoon paprika

1 teaspoon sea salt

MAKES ABOUT 6 TABLESPOONS

Put the whole spices and saffron threads into a dry skillet and toast over medium heat for about 1–2 minutes or until golden and aromatic. Let cool then transfer to a spice grinder (or clean coffee grinder) and crush to a coarse powder. Alternatively, use a mortar and pestle.

Put the spices into a bowl, add the remaining ingredients, and mix well. Set aside to infuse until ready to use.

fragrant Asian rub

4 whole star anise

2 teaspoons Szechuan peppercorns

1 teaspoon fennel seeds

2 small pieces of cassia bark or 1 cinnamon stick, broken

6 cloves

2 garlic cloves, finely chopped

grated zest of 2 unwaxed limes

1 teaspoon sea salt

MAKES ABOUT 6 TABLESPOONS

Put the whole spices into a dry skillet and toast over medium heat for 1–2 minutes or until golden and aromatic. Remove from the heat and let cool. Transfer to a spice grinder (or clean coffee grinder) and crush to a coarse powder. Alternatively, use a mortar and pestle.

Put the spices into a bowl, add the garlic, lime zest, and salt, and mix well. Set aside to infuse until ready to use.

corn and pepper salsa

2 large corn cobs

3 tablespoons safflower oil

4 scallions, trimmed and thinly sliced

freshly squeezed juice of 1 lime

6 small pickled peppers, finely chopped

2 tablespoons finely chopped fresh cilantro leaves

a dash of chili sauce or a large pinch of dried hot pepper flakes (optional)

sea salt and freshly ground black pepper

SERVES 4

Holding the corn cobs upright, cut down the sides with a sharp knife to remove the kernels. Heat a large skillet over medium heat and add 2 teaspoons of the oil. Stir-fry the corn for 2–3 minutes until it begins to brown. Add the scallions and stir-fry for 1 minute. Transfer to a bowl and let cool for 10 minutes.

Add the lime juice, peppers, cilantro, and the remaining oil, and mix well. Add a dash of chili sauce, if using, and season with salt and pepper.

salsa verde

4 heaping tablespoons finely chopped fresh flatleaf parsley

1 heaping tablespoon finely chopped fresh mint leaves

2 heaping tablespoons finely chopped fresh basil leaves

6 tablespoons extra virgin olive oil

2 tablespoons capers, rinsed and finely chopped

3 scallions, trimmed and finely chopped

2 garlic cloves, very finely chopped

2 tablespoons gherkins, rinsed and finely chopped

3 anchovy fillets, finely chopped

2 teaspoons Dijon mustard mixed with 2 tablespoons red wine vinegar

freshly ground black pepper

SERVES 4–6

Put the herbs in a bowl with half the olive oil. Stir, add the capers, scallions, garlic, gherkins, and anchovy fillets, and mix well. Add the mustard and vinegar mixture, then add enough of the remaining olive oil to make the salsa slightly sloppy. Season to taste with black pepper.

fresh tomato salsa

1 lb. ripe tomatoes, skinned and finely diced

½ red onion, finely chopped

1–2 small green chile peppers, seeded and finely chopped

3 tablespoons freshly squeezed lime juice

a pinch of sugar

2 tablespoons finely chopped cilantro

sea salt

SERVES 4

Put the tomatoes in a large bowl with the onion and chiles. Add the lime juice and mix well, then add the sugar and season with salt. When ready to serve, add the cilantro.

barbecue sauce

1 cup crushed tomatoes

½ cup maple syrup

2 tablespoons light molasses

2 tablespoons tomato ketchup

2 tablespoons white wine vinegar

3 tablespoons Worcestershire sauce

1 tablespoon Dijon mustard

1 teaspoon garlic powder

¼ teaspoon hot paprika

sea salt and freshly ground
black pepper

MAKES ABOUT 2 CUPS

Put all the ingredients into a small
saucepan, bring to a boil, and
simmer gently for 10–15 minutes
until reduced slightly and
thickened. Season to taste with
salt and pepper and let cool.

Pour into an airtight container
and store in the refrigerator for
up to 2 weeks.

sweet chile sauce

6 large red chile peppers, about
2 inches long, seeded and chopped

4 garlic cloves, chopped

1 teaspoon grated fresh ginger

1 teaspoon sea salt

½ cup rice wine vinegar

½ cup sugar

MAKES ABOUT 1 CUP

Put the chiles, garlic, ginger, and
salt into a food processor and
blend to a coarse paste. Transfer
to a saucepan, add the vinegar
and sugar, bring to a boil, and
simmer gently, part-covered,
for 5 minutes until the mixture
becomes a thin syrup. Remove
from the heat and let cool.

Pour into an airtight container
and store in the refrigerator for
up to 2 weeks.

Asian barbecue sauce

½ cup crushed tomatoes

2 tablespoons hoisin sauce

1 teaspoon hot chile sauce

2 garlic cloves, crushed

2 tablespoons sweet soy sauce

1 tablespoon rice wine vinegar

1 teaspoon ground coriander

½ teaspoon ground cinnamon

¼ teaspoon Chinese five-spice
powder

MAKES ABOUT 1½ CUPS

Put all the ingredients into a small
saucepan, add ½ cup water, bring
to a boil, and simmer gently for
10 minutes. Remove from the
heat and let cool.

Pour into an airtight container
and store in the refrigerator for
up to 2 weeks.

creamy corn salsa

1 corn cob, husk removed

2 red chile peppers, such as serrano

1 tomato, diced

1 garlic clove, crushed

freshly squeezed juice of ½ lime

1 tablespoon maple syrup

2 tablespoons sour cream

sea salt and freshly ground
black pepper

SERVES 6

Preheat an outdoor grill or broiler
until hot. Add the corn and cook
for about 15 minutes, turning
frequently, until charred on all
sides. Let cool.

Add the chile peppers and grill
until the skins are charred all over.
Transfer to a bowl and cover with
a clean cloth until cool.

Using a sharp knife, cut down all
sides of the corn cob to remove
the kernels. Put them into a bowl.
Peel and seed the chile peppers,
chop the flesh, and add it to the
corn in the bowl.

Stir in all the remaining ingredients,
season to taste, then serve.

hot pineapple and papaya salsa

½ ripe pineapple

½ large papaya

1–2 green chile peppers, such as
serrano, seeded and chopped

2 scallions, finely chopped

1 tablespoon chopped fresh mint

freshly squeezed juice of 1 lime

1 tablespoon Thai fish sauce

SERVES 6

Peel the pineapple, remove and
discard the core, then dice the
flesh and put into a serving bowl,
together with any juice.

Peel the papaya, scoop out the
seeds, and dice the flesh. Add
to the pineapple.

Stir in the chile peppers, scallions,
mint, lime juice, and fish sauce,
and set aside to infuse for about
30 minutes, then serve.

tomato, sesame, and ginger salsa

2 ripe tomatoes, peeled, seeded,
and diced

½ red onion, finely chopped

2-inch piece fresh ginger, peeled
and grated

1 garlic clove, chopped

1 tablespoon chopped fresh cilantro

2 tablespoons peanut oil

1 tablespoon soy sauce

1 teaspoon sesame oil

SERVES 6

Put all the ingredients into a
bowl, set aside to infuse for
about 30 minutes, then serve.

bell pepper butter sauce

Broiling the bell pepper until the skin chars makes it easier to peel and also gives the sauce a gorgeous smoky flavor.

1 large red bell pepper

5 tablespoons unsalted butter, diced

1 tablespoon freshly squeezed lime juice

a pinch of saffron threads

a pinch of cayenne pepper

sea salt and freshly ground black pepper

SERVES 4

Broil the bell pepper for 8–10 minutes, or until tender and charred all over. Seal in a plastic bag and leave until cool enough to handle.

Skin and seed the bell pepper, chop the flesh, and put in a saucepan with the butter, lime juice, saffron, and cayenne. Heat through until the butter has melted.

Using a food processor or hand blender, process the bell pepper mixture until smooth. Season to taste and heat through. Serve hot.

piri-piri sauce

Piri-piri is a condiment used in Portuguese cooking. It was introduced into Africa by the Portuguese, hence its Swahili name which translates as "chili" (or "chili-chili"). It is lovely drizzled over grilled chicken, or wonderful with char-grilled squid or shrimp.

8 red bird's eye chiles

1¼ cups extra virgin olive oil

1 tablespoon white wine vinegar

a pinch of sea salt

MAKES ABOUT 1¼ CUPS

Finely chop the chiles (including the seeds), put in a bowl, and add the olive oil, vinegar, and sea salt.

Transfer to a sterilized bottle (see page 39) and store in a cool place for up to 1 week.

smoky barbecue sauce

A good barbecue sauce should be tangy, smoky, and rich, just like this one. Serve in burgers or with grilled beef, lamb, or chicken.

¾ cup tomato purée

⅓ cup maple syrup

3 tablespoons dark molasses

3 tablespoons tomato ketchup

3 tablespoons malt vinegar

3 tablespoons Worcestershire sauce

1 tablespoon Dijon mustard

1 teaspoon garlic powder

a pinch of Spanish smoked paprika

sea salt and freshly ground black pepper

MAKES ABOUT 1⅔ CUPS

Put all the ingredients in a small saucepan, bring to a boil, and simmer gently for 10–15 minutes, or until reduced slightly, and thickened. Season to taste.

Pour into a sterilized bottle (see page 39) and refrigerate for up to 2 weeks.

Flavoring butter with herbs, spices, and aromatics provides a great staple to have on hand when grilling food. You can add an almost endless amount of flavorings to butter to serve with any type of meat, fish, or vegetables. Try the suggestions below or experiment with flavors of your own choice.

caper butter

2 tablespoons capers in brine, drained and patted dry

1 stick unsalted butter, softened

1 tablespoon chopped fresh flatleaf parsley

1 teaspoon finely grated lemon zest

freshly ground black pepper

SERVES 4–6

Finely chop the capers and put in a bowl with the butter, parsley, lemon zest, and pepper. Beat together with a fork until evenly combined.

Transfer the butter to a small piece of waxed paper and roll into a log. Wrap the paper around the butter and twist the ends to seal. Refrigerate or freeze until required. Serve in slices.

saffron butter

a large pinch of saffron threads

1 stick unsalted butter, softened

sea salt and freshly ground black pepper

SERVES 4–6

Soak the saffron in 1 teaspoon of boiling water for 10 minutes, then beat into the butter and season. Transfer to a small piece of waxed paper and continue to follow the recipe for caper butter.

herb butter

2 tablespoons chopped fresh herbs such as basil, chives, dill, mint, or parsley

1 stick unsalted butter, softened

sea salt and freshly ground black pepper

SERVES 4–6

Beat the herbs and seasoning into the butter until evenly combined. Transfer to a small piece of waxed paper and continue to follow the recipe for caper butter.

baba ganoush

3 eggplant

¼ cup plain yogurt

2 tablespoons tahini paste

1 garlic clove, crushed

1 teaspoon sea salt

freshly squeezed juice of 1–2 lemons, to taste

1 tablespoon finely chopped fresh flatleaf parsley (optional)

pita breads, warmed or lightly toasted, to serve

SERVES 8

Baba ganoush is the famous creamy eggplant purée with smoky overtones. It's best to char them over an open fire or outdoor grill to achieve the authentic smoky flavor, but, if you want to prepare it in advance, a hot broiler or the open flame on a gas stove are also fine. Serve baba ganoush as a dip or with other dishes as an appetizer.

Put the eggplant on the outdoor grill or over the open gas flame on top of the stove and cook until well charred on all sides. The steam created inside the vegetable will cook the flesh. The eggplant must be charred all over and soft in the middle. Remove from the flame and let cool on a plate.

When cool, carefully pull off the skins and stems. Don't leave any charred bits. Put the flesh into a bowl, then blend with a hand-held stick blender or potato masher: the texture should not be too smooth. Add the yogurt, tahini, garlic, and salt and blend again.

Add the juice of 1 lemon, taste, then gradually add more juice until you achieve flavor and texture to your taste. Transfer to a serving bowl and sprinkle with finely chopped parsley, if using.

Serve with wedges of toasted pita breads for scooping the dip.

tzatziki

½ cucumber, seeded and grated

2 teaspoons sea salt

1 garlic clove, crushed (optional)

⅔ cup Greek yogurt

freshly squeezed juice of ½ lemon

MAKES ABOUT 1 CUP

Greek tzatziki is a versatile dip that also makes a great salad dressing or accompaniment to grilled chicken and fish or vegetables.

Mix the grated cucumber and salt together and let stand for 10 minutes. Put the cucumber in the centre of a clean tea towel, gather up the edges, and twist to squeeze as much moisture out as possible. Put the cucumber in a bowl with the remaining ingredients and stir to combine. The tzatziki will keep in the refrigerator for 3 days.

Variations

Beet tzatziki Add 1 medium raw or 2 bottled beets, grated, and 2 tablespoons chopped chives to the mixture. This makes a great accompaniment to boiled new potatoes.

Spiced tzatziki Put 2 teaspoons cumin seeds and 2 teaspoons coriander seeds in a hot, dry skillet and heat, stirring continuously, for about 30 seconds until fragrant. Transfer to a mortar and pestle and grind to a powder. Add to the tzatziki along with 1 teaspoon paprika.

Olive tzatziki Stir ⅓–½ cup finely chopped stoned black or green olives into the yogurt and cucumber mixture.

guacamole

3 medium, ripe avocados, halved, pitted, and peeled

2 tablespoons freshly squeezed lime juice

1 small red onion, very finely chopped

1–2 green chile peppers, very finely chopped

1 tomato, seeded and finely chopped

sea salt

tortilla chips or bread sticks, to serve

MAKES ABOUT 2 CUPS

This popular Mexican dip can be made in many ways. This recipe contains all the popular ingredients, but feel free to leave out any you don't like. Adjust the chiles according to your taste.

Put the avocado flesh in a bowl with the lime juice and crush to a rough purée with a fork (if you like a smooth purée, you can blend the avocado and lime juice together in a food processor, then transfer to a bowl).

Add the onion, chiles, and tomato and mix until combined. Season to taste with salt. The guacamole will discolor quickly, so is best eaten on the day of making.

Variations

Herbed guacamole Add 2 teaspoons each of finely chopped cilantro, mint, and parsley to the guacamole for a pungent, refreshing dip.

Feta and avocado dip Add ½ cup finely crumbled feta cheese to the guacamole. This is great served with pita crisps.

parsley, feta, and pine nut dip

Flatleaf parsley leaves have such a delightful flavor, they make this dip beautifully fragrant. Serve with a selection of crisp raw vegetables or as an accompaniment to grilled fish.

2 handfuls fresh flatleaf parsley leaves

1 garlic clove, peeled and crushed

½ cup pine nuts, toasted

3½ oz. feta cheese, diced

⅓ cup extra virgin olive oil

freshly ground black pepper

SERVES 6–8

Put all the ingredients in a food processor and blend to form a fairly smooth sauce. Season to taste, cover, and set aside to infuse for 30 minutes before serving. Store in a screw-top jar in the refrigerator for up to 3 days.

chile tomato chutney

This versatile, tangy chutney is great with grilled meat or poultry.

1 small piece of dried chile, to taste

2-inch piece fresh ginger, peeled and coarsely chopped

2 garlic cloves

2 shallots

½ cup white wine vinegar

3 x 14-oz. cans whole plum tomatoes, drained, juice reserved, seeded, and chopped

1 cup light brown demerara sugar

MAKES 2 CUPS

Put the chile, ginger, garlic, and shallots in a food processor and chop finely. Put the vinegar, tomatoes, and sugar into a large, heavy saucepan, add the ginger mixture, and stir well.

Put the saucepan over medium heat, bring slowly to a boil, then simmer over low heat for 1½ hours or until reduced by half, stirring from time to time. Should the chutney dry out too much, add a little of the reserved tomato juice. Let cool a little, then spoon into a sterilized jam jar and seal with a screw-top lid.

Pictured on page 37, top right

peperonata

2 onions, thinly sliced

a large handful of fresh parsley, finely chopped, plus extra to serve

2 red bell peppers, seeded and sliced

2 yellow peppers, seeded and sliced

3 x 14-oz. cans whole plum tomatoes, drained, seeded, and chopped

sea salt and freshly ground black pepper

olive oil, for frying

SERVES 8

Cover the base of a heavy-based skillet with olive oil and put over medium heat. Add the onion and parsley and fry until the onion is softened, but not browned. Add the bell peppers, cook until soft, then add the tomatoes. Reduce the heat, cover, and cook for 1 hour, stirring from time to time. Season with salt and pepper to taste.

Serve hot or cold, sprinkled with parsley, with grilled meat, seafood, or poultry.

mango, kiwi, and cilantro salsa

1 large ripe mango, peeled, stoned, and cut into ½-inch cubes

4 kiwi fruit, peeled and cut into ½-inch cubes

finely grated zest and freshly squeezed juice of ½ unwaxed lemon

1 tablespoon extra virgin olive oil

1 tablespoon finely chopped fresh cilantro

sea salt and freshly ground black pepper

SERVES 4

Put the mango and kiwi fruit in a glass bowl, then add the lemon zest and juice, olive oil, and cilantro. Season with salt and pepper to taste and mix well. Cover and refrigerate until required. Serve with grilled seafood, chicken, or lamb.

parsley and anchovy relish

6 anchovy fillets

1 tablespoon salted capers, rinsed well and dried

a large handful of fresh parsley

grated zest of 1 unwaxed lemon

2 garlic cloves

¼ cup extra virgin olive oil

SERVES 4

Put the anchovies, capers, parsley, lemon zest, and garlic on a chopping board and chop together with a large kitchen knife so that all the ingredients remain identifiable but tiny. Alternatively, put the ingredients in a food processor and chop finely, but take care not to reduce them to a mush.

Transfer to a bowl and stir in the olive oil. Cover and refrigerate until required. Serve with grilled meat or fish.

tomato, lemon, and zucchini relish

2 small unwaxed lemons

1 lb. zucchini, finely chopped

2 red or white onions, finely chopped

4 tablespoons sea salt

2 lb. tomatoes, chopped

¾ cup sugar

1½ cups white wine vinegar or cider vinegar

1 tablespoon white mustard seeds

1 teaspoon dill seeds or celery seeds

¼ teaspoon turmeric

MAKES ABOUT 5 CUPS

Pickled or preserved lemons develop such a unique and wonderful flavor that is captured in this tomato and zucchini relish. It makes a great accompaniment to sausages, lamb, and chicken, but it really goes with practically anything!

Carefully cut the peel from the lemons, with a very thin layer of white pith. Finely chop and put in a glass or ceramic bowl with the juice from 1 of the lemons. Put the zucchini and onions in separate bowls. Sprinkle each with the salt, cover, and leave at room temperature overnight. When ready to make the relish, rinse well with cold water and drain thoroughly.

Put the tomatoes, sugar, and vinegar in a large saucepan and bring to a boil, stirring constantly to dissolve the sugar. Reduce to a simmer and cook for 1 hour, stirring occasionally, until thick. Bring back to a boil and add the drained lemon peel, zucchini, and onions with the mustard seeds, dill seeds, and turmeric. Cook for 5 minutes. Spoon into sterilized jars and seal. The relish will keep for up to 1 year if sealed correctly.

Note Always sterilize preserving jars before use. Wash them in hot, soapy water and rinse in boiling water. Place in a large saucepan and then cover with hot water. With the lid on, bring the water to a boil and continue boiling for 15 minutes. Turn off the heat, then leave the jars in the hot water until just before they are to be filled. Invert the jars onto paper towels to dry. Sterilize the lids for 5 minutes, by boiling, or according to the manufacturers' instructions. Jars should be filled and sealed while they are still hot.

sweet chile and tomato salsa

2 tablespoons sesame seeds

1 teaspoon Szechuan peppercorns

a small bunch of fresh cilantro, stems and leaves

3 garlic cloves, peeled

2 large, mild red chile peppers, stems removed

1¼-inch piece fresh ginger, peeled

½ cup sugar

2 tablespoons freshly squeezed lime juice

1 tablespoon soy sauce

4 tomatoes, chopped

MAKES ABOUT 1½ CUPS

This is an Asian-inspired salsa with a sweet and spicy flavor. It can be served as a dip with rice or prawn crackers or vegetable crisps, or as an accompaniment to grilled shellfish, fish, chicken, pork, or duck.

Heat a skillet to medium, add the sesame seeds, and toast, tossing the skillet, until golden. Set aside.

In the same skillet, toast the peppercorns for 3 minutes, stirring, until just fragrant. Let cool, transfer to a mortar and pestle, and roughly grind. Put the Szechuan pepper in a mini food processor with the cilantro stems, garlic, chiles, and ginger and process to a paste.

Put the sugar in a saucepan with a little water and bring to a boil, stirring until dissolved. Boil undisturbed for 1 minute, stir in the chile and ginger paste, and remove from the heat. Let cool.

In a bowl, mix together the sugar syrup and chile paste mixture, lime juice, soy sauce, chopped tomatoes, cilantro leaves, and sesame seeds. The salsa will keep in the refrigerator for 3 days.

chile jam

This fiery jam is a really useful ingredient to have in your pantry and it is so much better than the storebought varieties. It is hot, but the sweetness tempers this beautifully. It will store for a long time. Serve with Thai fishcakes or grilled shrimp.

2 lb. ripe tomatoes, roughly chopped

4 red bird's eye chiles, roughly chopped

2 garlic cloves, peeled

1 teaspoon grated fresh ginger

2 tablespoons light soy sauce

1 cup grated palm sugar

⅓ cup white wine vinegar

½ teaspoon sea salt

MAKES ABOUT 1¼ CUPS

Put the tomatoes, chiles, and garlic in a food processor and process until quite smooth. Transfer to a saucepan and add the remaining ingredients. Bring to a boil and simmer gently, stirring occasionally, for 30–40 minutes, or until thick and jam-like.

Spoon into a sterilized bottle or jar (see page 39) and leave to cool, then seal. Refrigerate once opened.

roast garlic, paprika, and sherry alioli

Creamy Spanish-style alioli is great as a dipping sauce for seafood and vegetables or a good accompaniment to grilled vegetables and meats.

1 whole garlic bulb

2 egg yolks

1 tablespoon sherry vinegar

¼ teaspoon sea salt

¼ teaspoon smoked paprika

⅔ cup light-flavored oil, such as grapeseed or vegetable

1 tablespoon sherry

MAKES ABOUT 1 CUP

Preheat the oven to 350°F.

Cut ½ inch off the top of the garlic bulb and discard. Loosely wrap the garlic in foil and roast in the preheated oven for 45 minutes until very soft. Let cool, then press the softened cloves from the skins. Crush the cloves on a chopping board with the side of a large knife to form a paste.

In a bowl, whisk together the garlic with the egg yolks, vinegar, salt, and paprika. Add the oil, drop by drop, whisking continuously until emulsified and thick. Finally whisk in the sherry. The alioli will keep in the refrigerator for 2–3 days.

4 lb. tomatoes

3 teaspoons sea salt

leaves from a small bunch
of fresh thyme

2 tablespoons olive oil

1 white onion, chopped

1 teaspoon whole allspice berries

½ teaspoon whole cloves

½ teaspoon black peppercorns

1 cup sugar

1 teaspoon dry mustard powder

2 cups cider vinegar

MAKES ABOUT 6 CUPS

roast tomato ketchup

Homemade tomato ketchup captures the true flavor of ripe tomatoes in season. Slow-roasting the tomatoes results in a more intense flavor, but one that is not as full-on as barbecue sauce.

Preheat the oven to 300°F.

Cut the tomatoes in half and arrange cut-side up in a roasting pan. Sprinkle with 2 teaspoons of the salt and all the thyme leaves and drizzle with 1 tablespoon of the oil. Roast in the preheated oven for 1½ hours.

Heat the remaining oil in a large saucepan over medium heat, add the onion, and sauté for 10 minutes until golden.

Put the allspice, cloves, and peppercorns in a mortar and pestle and grind to a powder. Add to the onion and cook for 1 minute. Add the roasted tomatoes, sugar, mustard powder, vinegar, and remaining teaspoon salt and bring to a boil. Adjust the heat to a steady low boil and cook for 30 minutes, uncovered, stirring occasionally to prevent burning.

Blend to a thick sauce using a stick blender or transfer to a blender. Transfer into sterilized bottles and seal (see note on page 39). The ketchup will keep for up to 1 year if properly sealed and stored in a cool, dark place.

meat dishes

cheeseburger

1½ lb. ground chuck

1 onion, finely chopped

1 garlic clove, crushed

2 teaspoons chopped fresh thyme

4 oz. Cheddar cheese, sliced

4 burger buns, halved

4 tablespoons Mayonnaise
(see page 199)

4 large leaves of butterhead
lettuce

2 tomatoes, sliced

½ red onion, thinly sliced

sea salt and freshly ground
black pepper

olive oil, for brushing

SERVES 4

This version of a cheeseburger avoids the usual processed cheese slices in favor of a good-quality cheese—and tastes all the better for it. You can vary the cheese to your own taste—whether a traditional Cheddar or, if you are feeling adventurous, a Camembert or crumbled Roquefort.

Put the beef, onion, garlic, thyme, and some salt and pepper in a bowl and work together with your hands until evenly mixed and slightly sticky. Divide into 4 portions and shape into patties. Cover and chill for 30 minutes.

Preheat the grill. Brush the patties lightly with olive oil and grill for 5 minutes on each side until lightly charred and cooked through. Top the patties with the cheese slices and set under a hot broiler for 30 seconds until the cheese has melted. Keep them warm.

Toast the buns, then spread each base and top with mayonnaise. Add the lettuce leaves, cheese-topped patties, and tomato and onion slices. Add the bun tops and serve hot.

Kids love burgers and these are served as sausage shapes in a hot dog roll. Alternatively, shape as the more traditional patties and serve in small toasted buns. You can add some shredded lettuce and tomatoes to the burger for a healthier option.

"sausage" burgers for kids

1 lb. prime ground beef

2 teaspoons onion powder

2 tablespoons Roast Tomato Ketchup (page 44 or you can use store-bought ketchup), plus extra to serve

2 tablespoons chopped fresh flatleaf parsley

8 hot dog rolls

½ cup grated Cheddar cheese

sea salt and freshly ground black pepper

olive oil, for brushing

SERVES 4

Put the beef, onion powder, tomato ketchup, parsley, and a little salt and pepper in a bowl and work together with your hands until evenly mixed. Divide into 4 portions and mold into long thin sausage shapes. Cover and chill for 30 minutes.

Brush the "sausage" burgers lightly with olive oil and cook on a preheated grill for 7–8 minutes, turning frequently until lightly charred and cooked through.

Split the rolls horizontally without cutting all the way through. Put a "sausage" into each one and sprinkle with some grated cheese and tomato ketchup. Serve hot.*

open Tex-Mex burger
with chile relish

1½ lb. ground chuck

1 small red onion, finely chopped

1 garlic clove, crushed

2 teaspoons dried oregano

1½ teaspoons ground cumin

2 burger buns, halved

1 cup shredded iceberg lettuce

¼ cup grated Cheddar cheese

sea salt and freshly ground
black pepper

olive oil, for brushing

Chile relish

1 lb. tomatoes, coarsely chopped

1 red onion, coarsely chopped

2 garlic cloves, crushed

2–4 jalapeño chile peppers,
coarsely chopped

2 tablespoons
Worcestershire sauce

1 cup soft brown sugar

⅔ cup red wine vinegar

2 teaspoons sea salt

SERVES 4

The flavors of Texas and Mexico combine well in this tangy burger. For those who really like it hot, try the Caribbean version with the fiery chile sauce.

To make the chile relish, put the tomatoes, onion, garlic, and chiles in a food processor and blend until smooth. Transfer the mixture to a saucepan, add the Worcestershire sauce, sugar, vinegar, and the 2 teaspoons of salt. Bring to a boil and simmer gently for 30–40 minutes until the sauce has thickened. Let cool completely and refrigerate until required.

Put the beef, onion, garlic, oregano, cumin, and some salt and pepper in a bowl and work together with your hands until slightly sticky and evenly mixed. Divide into 4 portions and shape into patties. Cover and chill for 30 minutes.

Preheat the grill. Brush the patties lightly with olive oil and cook for 4–5 minutes on each side until lightly charred and cooked through. Keep them warm.

Lightly toast the buns. Top each half with shredded lettuce, a patty, some grated cheese, and chile relish. Serve hot.

Variation

Caribbean Chile Burger Make the chile relish as above, but replace the jalapeño chiles with 1 Scotch bonnet or habanero chile, seeded and chopped. When assembling the burger, add a layer of sliced avocado to help to temper the fire of the extra-hot chile sauce (use disposable latex gloves when handling Scotch bonnet or habanero chiles).

Beef satay

1 lb. beef sirloin, sliced against the grain into bite-sized pieces

1 tablespoon peanut oil

Peanut sauce

¼ cup peanut or vegetable oil

4–5 garlic cloves, crushed

4–5 dried serrano chile peppers, seeded and ground using a pestle and mortar

1–2 teaspoons curry powder

½ cup roasted peanuts, finely ground

To serve

a small bunch of fresh cilantro

a small bunch of fresh mint

lime wedges

a packet of short wooden or bamboo skewers, soaked in water before use

SERVES 4–6

fiery beef satay
in peanut sauce

Beef, pork, or chicken satays cooked in, or served with, a fiery peanut sauce are hugely popular throughout Southeast Asia. This particular sauce is a great favorite in Thailand, Vietnam, and Indonesia. It is best to make your own but commercial brands are available under the banner satay or sate sauce.

To make the sauce, heat the oil in a heavy-based saucepan and stir in the garlic until it begins to color. Add the chiles, curry powder, and the peanuts and stir over a gentle heat, until the mixture forms a paste. Remove from the heat and leave to cool.

Put the beef pieces in a bowl. Beat the peanut oil into the sauce and tip the mixture onto the beef. Mix well, so that the beef is evenly coated, and thread the meat onto the prepared skewers.

Cook the satays on a preheated grill for 2–3 minutes on each side, then serve the skewered meat with the lime wedges and fresh herbs to wrap around each tasty morsel.

spicy beef and coconut kofta kabobs

1 teaspoon coriander seeds

1 teaspoon cumin seeds

1⅓ cups dried shredded or freshly grated coconut, plus 2–3 tablespoons, to serve

1 tablespoon coconut oil

4 shallots, peeled and finely chopped

2 garlic cloves, finely chopped

1–2 fresh red chile peppers, seeded and finely chopped

12 oz. lean ground beef

1 beaten egg, to bind

sea salt and freshly ground black pepper

lime wedges, to serve

a packet of short wooden or bamboo skewers, soaked in water before use

SERVES 4

Variations of this Asian dish can be found at street stalls from Sri Lanka to the Philippines and South Africa to the West Indies. Simple and tasty, the kofta are delicious grilled and served with wedges of fresh lime or a dipping sauce of your choice.

In a small heavy-based skillet, dry roast the coriander and cumin seeds until they give off a nutty aroma. Using a mortar and pestle, or a spice grinder, grind the roasted seeds to a powder.

In the same skillet, dry roast the coconut until it begins to color and give off a nutty aroma. Tip it onto a plate to cool, reserving 2–3 tablespoons.

Heat the coconut oil in the same skillet and stir in the shallots, garlic, and chiles, until fragrant and beginning to color. Tip them onto a plate to cool.

Put the ground beef in a bowl and add the ground spices, toasted coconut, and shallot mixture. Season with salt and pepper and use a fork to mix all the ingredients together, adding a little egg to bind it (you may not need it all). Knead the mixture with your hands and mold it into little balls. Thread the balls onto the prepared skewers.

Prepare a charcoal grill. Cook the kabobs for 3–4 minutes on each side. Sprinkle the cooked kofta with the reserved toasted coconut and serve with the wedges of lime to squeeze over them.

Tuscan-style steak

1 large T-bone steak, about 1¾ lb. and cut to an even thickness of 1–1¼ inches

6 tablespoons olive oil

2 garlic cloves, thinly sliced

3 sprigs of fresh rosemary

sea salt and freshly ground black pepper

good-quality extra virgin olive oil, for drizzling

To serve

sautéed potatoes

arugula salad

lemon wedges (optional)

SERVES 2

The traditional cut to use for this classic Tuscan recipe, known locally as Bistecca alla Fiorentina, is a T-bone steak, marinated overnight in olive oil and garlic and cooked over a charcoal grill. You could also use a gas grill—either way, it's a treat for any meat lover!

Trim the excess fat off the edge of the steak, leaving a little if liked, and pat the steak dry with paper towels. Pour the measured olive oil into a shallow dish and add the garlic and rosemary. Turn the steak in the oil, ensuring there is some garlic and rosemary on each side. Cover with a double layer of plastic wrap and let marinate in the refrigerator for 24 hours, turning a couple of times. Bring to room temperature before cooking it.

Preheat a charcoal grill. Take the meat out of the marinade and remove any pieces of garlic or rosemary from the steak. Pat dry with paper towels. Put the steak on a rack about 3 inches above the coals and cook for about 4 minutes. Turn the steak over and cook for a further 3 minutes. (Cook for a couple of minutes longer on each side for a medium-rare steak, although this is traditionally served rare.)

Transfer to a warm plate and season both sides with salt and pepper. Cover lightly with aluminum foil, then let rest for 5 minutes.

Stand the steak upright with the bone at the bottom and, using a sharp knife, remove the meat either side of the bone in one piece. Cut the meat into slices, ¼–½ inch thick. Divide the slices between 2 serving plates. Pour over any meat juices that have accumulated under the meat and drizzle with the best extra virgin olive oil you can lay your hands on.

Serve with sautéed potatoes, an arugula salad, and lemon wedges.

Argentinian-style "asado" steak with chimichurri salsa

a whole piece of sirloin, 3–4 lb.

olive oil, for rubbing and brushing

sea salt

roasted new potatoes*, to serve

green salad, to serve

Chimichurri salsa

⅔ cup olive oil

⅓ cup red wine vinegar

1 teaspoon dried oregano

4–5 tablespoons chopped fresh flatleaf parsley, stalks removed and chopped

½–1 teaspoon crushed dried chiles

2 large garlic cloves, finely chopped

1 bay leaf

⅔ cup salmuera (salt water solution made from 1 heaping tablespoon sea salt dissolved in ⅔ cup warm water and cooled)

SERVES 8–10

Serve juicy steak Argentinian style with the classic accompaniment of chimichurri salsa—a punchy, garlic dressing that needs to be made the day before for the flavors to fully develop.

To make the chimichurri salsa, put the olive oil, vinegar, oregano, parsley, crushed dried chiles, garlic, bay leaf, and salmuera in a screw-top jar and shake well. Chill overnight in the refrigerator. Bring to room temperature before serving.

Trim the meat of excess fat, then rub lightly with olive oil, and sprinkle with salt. Preheat a charcoal grill and let it burn until the flames have completely died down and the ash is a powdery white. Put the beef on a rack 3 inches above the hot coals. Cook for 15–20 minutes for a rare steak or 25–30 minutes for a medium-rare steak, turning every 4–5 minutes. If the meat seems to be drying out, brush over a little extra oil. Transfer to a warm plate, cover lightly with aluminum foil, and let rest for 5–10 minutes.

Cut the steak into thick slices and serve a couple of slices on each plate. Shake the chimichurri salsa vigorously and splash over the steaks. Serve with roasted new potatoes and a green salad.

*Note To make roasted new potatoes, put 2 lb. halved new potatoes in a roasting pan with 5 tablespoons olive oil, 4 sprigs of fresh rosemary, and 6–8 garlic cloves. Roast in a preheated oven at 350°F for about 45 minutes, turning occasionally.

Steak and blue cheese complement each other perfectly as the cheese brings out the taste of the beef. This dish is made even more special when combined with the smoky char-grilled flavors of an outdoor grill.

4 top loin or tenderloin steaks, 8 oz. each

sea salt and freshly ground black pepper

baby spinach salad, to serve

Blue cheese butter

4 tablespoons butter, softened

2 oz. soft blue cheese, such as Gorgonzola

¼ cup walnuts, finely ground in a blender

2 tablespoons chopped fresh parsley

sea salt and freshly ground black pepper

SERVES 4

steak with blue cheese butter

To make the blue cheese butter, put the butter, cheese, walnuts, and parsley into a bowl and beat well. Season to taste. Form into a log, wrap in a piece of waxed paper, twist the ends to seal, and chill for about 30 minutes.

Lightly season the steaks and cook on a preheated grill (or sauté in a little oil in a skillet) for 3 minutes on each side for rare, or 4–5 minutes for medium to well done.

Cut the butter into 8 slices. Put 2 slices of butter onto each cooked steak, wrap loosely with foil, and let rest for 5 minutes.

Serve the steaks with a salad of baby spinach.

2 long, thin pieces of bavette (skirt steak), about 6–7 oz. each, or 12–14 oz. bottom round steak

8 flour tortillas

crisp romaine lettuce leaves, shredded

Marinade

3 tablespoons freshly squeezed lime juice

1 garlic clove, crushed

1 teaspoon mild chile powder

3 tablespoons light olive oil

Chunky guacamole

2 large avocados, about 7 oz. each

2 tablespoons freshly squeezed lime juice

4 scallions, trimmed and thinly sliced

1 garlic clove, crushed

1 small green chile pepper, seeded and thinly sliced (optional)

1 tablespoon olive oil

2–3 tomatoes, about 6 oz., skinned, seeded, and chopped

3 tablespoons chopped cilantro leaves

sea salt

SERVES 4

char-grilled steak fajitas
with chunky guacamole

The word fajitas, meaning straps, actually refers to the cut of beef that is traditionally used for this classic Tex-Mex dish, which is cooked over an open fire. If you want to use the authentic cut, a skirt steak, you'll probably need to order it from a butcher in advance.

To make the marinade, put the lime juice, garlic, and chile powder in a shallow dish and whisk together. Gradually whisk in the olive oil. Put the steaks in the marinade and turn so that they are thoroughly coated. Cover and let marinate for 30 minutes while you prepare and light an outdoor grill.

Meanwhile, to make the guacamole, scoop out the flesh from the avocados and put it in a bowl with the lime juice. Chop with a knife to give a chunky consistency. Add the scallions, garlic, chile, if using, and olive oil and mix well. Add the tomatoes, cilantro, and salt, cover, and set aside.

When the flames have completely died down and ash is powdery white, pat the steak dry with paper towels and cook for about 1½ minutes each side. Set aside and let rest for 3–4 minutes while you warm the tortillas in a dry skillet. Thinly slice the steak, then put a dollop of guacamole on each tortilla and top with slices of steak and shredded lettuce leaves. Carefully roll up the tortillas, press together, and cut in half diagonally.

lamb burgers
with mint yogurt

1½ lb. boneless lamb shoulder, cut into ½–inch cubes

4 oz. salt pork, chopped

1 onion, very finely chopped

2 garlic cloves, crushed

2 tablespoons ground cumin

2 teaspoons ground cinnamon

1 tablespoon dried oregano

2 teaspoons sea salt

½ cup fresh breadcrumbs

1 tablespoon capers, drained and chopped

1 extra large egg, beaten

freshly ground black pepper

Mint yogurt

8 oz. plain yogurt

2 tablespoons chopped fresh mint

sea salt and freshly ground black pepper

To serve

4 crusty rolls

salad leaves

tomato slices

SERVES 4

A good burger should be thick, moist, tender, and juicy. These lamb burgers are all that and more. Serve in crusty rolls with a few slices of tomato, plenty of fresh salad leaves, and a generous spoonful of the cool minty yogurt dressing. The perfect burger for a patio picnic.

Put the lamb and pork into a food processor and process briefly until coarsely ground. Transfer to a bowl and, using your hands, work in the chopped onion, garlic, cumin, cinnamon, oregano, salt, breadcrumbs, capers, beaten egg, and pepper. Cover and let marinate in the refrigerator for at least 2 hours.

Put the yogurt into a bowl and stir in the mint, then add a little salt and pepper to taste. Set aside until required.

Using damp hands, shape the meat into 8 burgers. Preheat the grill, then brush the grill rack with oil. Cook the burgers for about 3 minutes on each side.

Split the rolls in half and fill with the cooked burgers, salad leaves, tomato slices, and a spoonful of mint yogurt.

Variation

For a traditional hamburger, replace the lamb with beef, omit the spices, and, instead of the capers, add 4 chopped anchovy fillets. Serve in burger buns with salad.

1.5–2 kg leg of lamb, butterflied

1 recipe Herb, Lemon, and Garlic Marinade (page 15)

1 recipe Salsa Verde (page 19), to serve

White bean salad

1 large red onion, finely chopped

3 x 14-oz. cans white or cannellini beans, drained

2 garlic cloves, chopped

3 tomatoes, seeded and chopped

⅓ cup extra virgin olive oil

1½ tablespoons red wine vinegar

2 tablespoons chopped fresh parsley

sea salt and freshly ground black pepper

SERVES 8

butterflied lamb
with white bean salad

This is probably the best way to cook lamb on the grill —the bone is removed and the meat opened out flat so it can cook quickly and evenly over the coals. If you don't fancy boning the lamb yourself, ask the butcher to do it for you.

To make the salad, put the onion into a colander, sprinkle with salt, and let drain over a bowl for 30 minutes. Wash the onion under cold running water and dry well. Transfer to a bowl, then add the beans, garlic, tomatoes, olive oil, vinegar, parsley, and salt and pepper to taste.

Put the lamb into a shallow dish, pour over the marinade, cover, and let marinate in the refrigerator overnight. Remove from the refrigerator 1 hour before cooking.

Preheat the grill. Drain the lamb and discard the marinade. Cook over medium hot coals for 12–15 minutes on each side until lightly charred on the outside but still pink in the middle (cook for a little longer if you prefer the meat less rare). Let the lamb rest for 10 minutes.

Cut the lamb into slices and serve with the white bean salad and salsa verde.

2 lb. boneless lamb, such
as shoulder

1 tablespoon chopped
fresh rosemary

1 tablespoon dried oregano

1 onion, chopped

4 garlic cloves, chopped

1¼ cups red wine

freshly squeezed juice of 1 lemon

⅓ cup olive oil

sea salt and freshly ground
black pepper

Cracked wheat salad

3¼ cups cracked wheat
(bulgur wheat)

1 cup chopped fresh parsley

½ cup fresh mint leaves

2 garlic cloves, crushed

½ cup extra virgin olive oil

freshly squeezed juice of 2 lemons

a pinch of sugar

sea salt and freshly ground
black pepper

*6 large rosemary stalks or
metal skewers*

SERVES 6

souvlaki with
cracked wheat salad

**Souvlaki is the classic Greek kabob, a delicious
combination of cubed lamb marinated in red wine with
herbs and lemon juice. The meat is tenderized by the
wine, resulting in a juicy and succulent dish.**

Trim any large pieces of fat from the lamb and then cut the meat
into 1-inch cubes. Put into a shallow, non-metal dish. Add the
rosemary, oregano, onion, garlic, wine, lemon juice, olive oil,
salt, and pepper. Toss well, cover and leave to marinate in the
refrigerator for 4 hours. Return to room temperature for 1 hour
before cooking.

To make the salad, soak the cracked wheat in warm water for
30 minutes until the water has been absorbed and the grains have
softened. Strain well to extract any excess water and transfer the
wheat to a bowl. Add all the remaining ingredients, season to
taste, and set aside for 30 minutes to develop the flavors.

Thread the lamb onto large rosemary stalks or metal skewers.
Cook on a preheated outdoor grill for 10 minutes, turning and
basting from time to time. Leave to rest for 5 minutes, then
serve with the salad.

1 lb. finely ground lean lamb

1 onion, grated

2 teaspoons ground cumin

1 teaspoon ground coriander

1 teaspoon paprika

½–1 teaspoon cayenne pepper

1 teaspoon sea salt

a small bunch of fresh flatleaf parsley, finely chopped

a small bunch of fresh cilantro, finely chopped

leafy herb salad, to serve

flatbreads, to serve

Hot hummus

1½ cups dried chickpeas, soaked overnight and cooked in plenty of water until tender, or a 14-oz. can cooked chickpeas, drained

3 tablespoons olive oil

freshly squeezed juice of 1 lemon

1 teaspoon cumin seeds

2 tablespoons light tahini

4 tablespoons thick, strained plain yogurt

sea salt and freshly ground black pepper

2½ tablespoons butter

2 metal skewers with wide, flat blades

SERVES 4–6

cumin-flavored lamb kabobs with hot hummus

Typical fodder at the street grills or kabob houses, these kabobs are enjoyed throughout the Middle East and North Africa. To prepare them successfully, you will need large metal skewers with wide, flat blades to hold the meat.

Mix the ground lamb with the other ingredients and knead well. Pound the meat to a smooth consistency in a large mortar and pestle, or whizz in a food processor. Leave to sit for an hour to let the flavors mingle.

Meanwhile, make the hummus. Preheat the oven to 400°F. In a food processor, whizz the chickpeas with the olive oil, lemon juice, cumin seeds, tahini, and yogurt. Season to taste, tip the mixture into an ovenproof dish, cover with foil, and put in the preheated oven to warm through.

Wet your hands to make the meat mixture easier to handle. Mold portions of the mixture around the skewers, squeezing and flattening it, so it looks like the sheath to a sword.

Preheat the outdoor grill. Cook the kabobs for 4–5 minutes on each side. Quickly melt the butter in a saucepan or in the microwave and pour it over the hummus. When the kabobs are cooked on both sides, slip the meat off the skewers, cut into bite-sized pieces, and serve with the hot hummus, a leafy herb salad, and flatbreads on the side.

1 lb. tender lamb, from the leg or shoulder, cut into bite-sized chunks

2 tablespoons olive oil

freshly squeezed juice of 1–2 lemons

leaves from a bunch of fresh sage, finely chopped (reserve a few whole leaves)

2 garlic cloves, crushed

sea salt and freshly ground black pepper

4–8 fresh medium-sized porcini, cut into quarters or thickly sliced

To serve

truffle oil, to drizzle

Parmesan cheese shavings

grilled or toasted sourdough bread

4 long, thin metal skewers

SERVES 4

lamb and porcini kabobs
with sage and parmesan

Rural feasts in Italy often involve grilling outdoors. One of the most exciting times is the mushroom season when entire villages hunt for wild mushrooms and gather together to cook them. These kabobs are prepared with fresh porcini, but you could substitute them with dried porcini reconstituted in water or field mushrooms.

Put the lamb pieces in a bowl and toss in the oil and lemon juice. Add the sage and garlic and season with salt and pepper. Cover, refrigerate, and leave to marinate for about 2 hours.

Thread the lamb onto skewers adding a quarter, or slice, of porcini every so often with a sage leaf. Brush with any of the marinade left in the bowl. Prepare a charcoal grill. Cook the kabobs for 3–4 minutes on each side.

Serve immediately with a drizzle of truffle oil, Parmesan shavings, and toasted sourdough bread, if liked.

1 lb. ground lean lamb

2 onions, finely chopped

1 fresh green chile pepper, finely chopped

4 garlic cloves, crushed

1 teaspoon paprika

1 teaspoon ground sumac (see note on page 147)

leaves from a small bunch of fresh flatleaf parsley, finely chopped

Sauce

2 tablespoons olive oil plus a nut of butter

1 onion, finely chopped

2 garlic cloves, finely chopped

1 fresh green chile pepper, seeded and finely chopped

1 teaspoon sugar

14-oz. can chopped tomatoes

sea salt and freshly ground black pepper

To serve

8 plum tomatoes

2 tablespoons butter

1 large pide or plain naan bread, cut into pieces

1 teaspoon ground sumac

1 teaspoon dried oregano

1 cup thick plain yogurt

a bunch of fresh flatleaf parsley, chopped

1 large metal skewer with a wide, flat blade, plus 1 long thin skewer

SERVES 4

lamb shish kabob
with yogurt and flatbread

There are variations of shish kabobs throughout the Middle East but this tasty Turkish version, designed to use up day-old "pide" bread, is outstanding.

Put the ground lamb in a bowl. Add all the other kabob ingredients and knead well, until it resembles a smooth paste and is quite sticky. Cover and chill in the refrigerator for about 15 minutes.

To make the sauce, heat the oil and butter in a heavy-based saucepan. Add the onion, garlic, and chile, and stir until they begin to color. Add the sugar and tomatoes and cook, uncovered, until quite thick. Season to taste. Keep warm.

Wet your hands to make the meat mixture easier to handle. Mold portions of the mixture around the large skewer, squeezing and flattening it, so it looks like the sheath to the sword. Thread the plum tomatoes onto the thin skewer.

Preheat the charcoal grill. Cook the kabob for 4–5 minutes on each side. Add the tomatoes to the grill and cook until charred and soft. While both are cooking, melt the butter in a heavy-based skillet, add the pide pieces, and toss until golden. Sprinkle with some of the sumac and oregano and arrange on a serving plate. Spoon some sauce and half the yogurt on top.

When the kabob is cooked on both sides, slip the meat off the skewer, cut into pieces, and arrange on top of the pide along with the tomatoes. Sprinkle with salt and the remaining sumac and oregano. Add more sauce and yogurt and garnish with parsley.

top dogs

This hot dog recipe calls for good-quality pork sausages—buy the best you can find—which are delicious combined with the caramelized onions and whole-grain mustard.

2 onions, cut into thin wedges

2–3 tablespoons extra virgin olive oil

1 tablespoon chopped fresh sage

sea salt and freshly ground black pepper

4 natural casing frankfurters or bratwursts, pricked

4 hot dog buns

4 tablespoons whole-grain mustard

2 ripe tomatoes, sliced

SERVES 4

Put the onion wedges into a bowl, add the olive oil, sage, and a little salt and pepper and mix well. Preheat the flat plate on the gas grill and cook the onions for 15–20 minutes, stirring occasionally until golden and tender. If you have a charcoal grill, cook the onions in a skillet on top of the grill. Keep hot.

Meanwhile, cook the frankfurters or bratwursts over hot coals for 10–12 minutes, turning frequently until charred and cooked through. Transfer to a plate and let rest briefly.

Cut the rolls almost in half, then put onto the grill rack and toast for a few minutes. Remove from the heat and spread with mustard. Fill with the tomatoes, sausages, and onions.

1½ lb. ground pork

2 garlic cloves, crushed

1 teaspoon grated fresh ginger

2 tablespoons chopped
fresh cilantro

2 tablespoons cornstarch

1 egg, lightly beaten

4 hero rolls

a handful of fresh herbs, such as
Thai or plain basil, cilantro, and
mint leaves

sea salt and freshly ground
black pepper

peanut or safflower oil, for
brushing

Satay sauce

4 tablespoons chunky
peanut butter

2 tablespoons coconut cream

2 tablespoons freshly squeezed
lime juice

1 tablespoon sweet chile sauce,
plus extra to serve

2 teaspoons light soy sauce

1 teaspoon soft brown sugar

*12 wooden or bamboo skewers,
soaked in water before use*

SERVES 4

spiced pork burger
with satay sauce

**This burger is inspired by some of the wonderful pork
skewers served in Thai restaurants, with their great
use of fresh herbs and satay sauce.**

Put the pork, garlic, ginger, cilantro, cornstarch, egg, salt, and
pepper to taste in a bowl and work together with your hands until
evenly mixed. Divide into 12 portions and shape into small logs.
Cover and chill for 30 minutes.

Meanwhile, to make the satay sauce, put the peanut butter,
coconut cream, lime juice, chile sauce, soy sauce, and brown
sugar in a small saucepan and heat gently, stirring until mixed.
Simmer gently for 1–2 minutes until thickened. Set aside to cool.

Thread the patties onto the soaked skewers and brush with oil.
Grill for 6–8 minutes, turning frequently, until charred on the
outside and cooked through. Keep them warm.

To serve, split the rolls down the middle, open out, and fill with
herbs. Remove the skewers from the pork patties and add the
patties to the rolls along with some satay sauce and sweet chile
sauce. Serve hot.

aromatic pork burger in pita bread with chile tomato chutney

3 slices white bread

5 tablespoons milk

1¾ lb. ground pork

2 eggs

a handful of fresh parsley, finely chopped

4 garlic cloves, crushed

1 teaspoon ground cinnamon

a large pinch of ground cloves

1 teaspoon ground turmeric

a large pinch of chili powder

the seeds of 4 cardamom pods, crushed

1 teaspoon sea salt

freshly ground black pepper

olive oil, for brushing

Yogurt dressing

10 oz. plain yogurt

the seeds of 8 cardamom pods, crushed

a large pinch of sea salt

To serve

Chile Tomato Chutney (page 35)

6 pita breads

2 cups shredded iceberg lettuce

SERVES 4–6

No cook-out is complete without burgers, but burgers don't necessarily have to mean junk food. Not only is it healthier to make your own, but fun too as you can experiment with herbs and spices to suit your own taste.

To make the yogurt dressing, put the yogurt and cardamom seeds in a small bowl, add the salt, and mix well. Cover and refrigerate until required.

Soak the bread in the milk for 10–15 minutes until soft, then squeeze the bread with your hands until it is almost dry and put in a bowl. Add the ground pork, eggs, parsley, garlic, spices, salt, and plenty of pepper. Mix well, cover, and leave to stand for 1 hour.

Shape the meat mixture into 12 patties. Cover and refrigerate until required.

When ready to cook, brush the patties lightly with olive oil and cook them on a preheated hot grill for 20 minutes, turning them from time to time to avoid burning. Cut into one of the burgers to make sure it is cooked in the middle—if it is still pink, cook for an extra 5–10 minutes. Alternatively, cook the burgers in a skillet over medium heat for 20 minutes, or put them in an oiled roasting pan and cook in a preheated oven at 350°F for 20–30 minutes, turning from time to time. Transfer the burgers to a plate and spread each one with a spoonful of chile tomato chutney.

Heat the pita breads on the grill or in the oven until just warm. Cut each one in half, open, and fill with lettuce, yogurt dressing, and a burger, then serve.

Vietnamese pork balls

1 lemongrass stalk

1¼ lb. ground pork

⅓ cup breadcrumbs

6 kaffir lime leaves, very finely sliced

2 garlic cloves, crushed

1-inch piece fresh ginger, peeled and grated

1 fresh red hot chile, seeded and chopped

2 tablespoons Thai fish sauce

To serve

lettuce leaves

a handful of fresh herb leaves, such as mint, cilantro, and Thai basil

Sweet Chile Sauce (page 20)

4 wooden or bamboo skewers, soaked in water before use

SERVES 4

Like many Vietnamese dishes, these delicious pork balls are served wrapped in a lettuce leaf with plenty of fresh herbs and Sweet Chile Sauce.

Using a sharp knife, trim the lemongrass stalk to about 6 inches, then remove and discard the tough outer leaves. Chop the inner stalk very finely.

Put the ground pork and breadcrumbs into a bowl, then add the lemongrass, lime leaves, garlic, ginger, chile, and fish sauce and mix well. Let marinate in the refrigerator for at least 1 hour.

Using your hands, shape the mixture into 20 small balls and carefully thread 5 onto each of the soaked wooden skewers. Preheat the grill, then brush the grill rack with oil. Cook the skewers over hot coals for 5–6 minutes, turning halfway through until cooked.

Serve the pork balls wrapped in the lettuce leaves with the herbs and sweet chile sauce.

1 lb. pork tenderloin, cut into bite-sized cubes or strips

Marinade

4 shallots, peeled and chopped

4 garlic cloves, peeled

2–3 teaspoons curry powder

2 tablespoons dark soy sauce

2 tablespoons sesame or peanut oil

Pineapple sauce

4 shallots, peeled and chopped

2 garlic cloves, chopped

4 dried red chiles, soaked in warm water until soft, seeded, and chopped

1 lemongrass stalk, trimmed and chopped

1-inch piece fresh ginger, peeled and chopped

2 tablespoons sesame or peanut oil

¾ cup coconut milk

2 teaspoons tamarind paste (see note on page 160)

2 teaspoons sugar

1 small fresh pineapple, peeled, cored and cut into slices

sea salt

a packet of short wooden or bamboo skewers, soaked in water before use

SERVES 4

curried pork satay
with pineapple sauce

This spicy satay is popular in Malaysia and Singapore. A combination of Indian, Malay, and Chinese traditions, it is best accompanied by a rice pilaf or chunks of bread.

To make the marinade, use a mortar and pestle, or a food processor, to pound the shallots and garlic to form a paste. Stir in the curry powder and soy sauce, and bind with the oil. Rub the marinade into the meat, making sure it is well coated. Cover and refrigerate for at least 2 hours.

In the meantime, prepare the sauce. Using a mortar and pestle, or a food processor, pound the shallots, garlic, chiles, lemongrass, and ginger to form a paste. Heat the oil in a heavy-based pan and stir in the paste. Cook for 2–3 minutes until fragrant and beginning to color, then stir in the coconut milk, tamarind, and sugar. Bring the mixture to a boil, then reduce the heat and simmer for about 5 minutes. Season to taste and leave to cool. Using a mortar and pestle, or a food processor, crush 3 slices of the fresh pineapple and beat them into the sauce.

Preheat the grill. Thread the marinated meat onto the prepared skewers. Line them up over the hot charcoal and place the remaining slices of pineapple beside them. Char the pineapple slices and chop them into chunks. Grill the meat until just cooked, roughly 2–3 minutes each side, and serve immediately with the charred pineapple chunks for spearing, and the pineapple sauce for dipping.

2 teaspoons peanut or sesame oil

4 shallots, finely chopped

2 garlic cloves, finely chopped

1 lb. ground pork

2 tablespoons Thai fish sauce

2 teaspoons Chinese five-spice powder

2 teaspoons sugar

2 handfuls of fresh white or brown breadcrumbs

sea salt and freshly ground black pepper

noodles, to serve

Sweet and sour sauce

2 teaspoons peanut oil

1 garlic clove, finely chopped

1 fresh red chile pepper, seeded and finely chopped

2 tablespoons roasted peanuts, finely chopped

1 tablespoon Thai fish sauce

2 tablespoons rice wine vinegar

2 tablespoons hoisin sauce

4 tablespoons coconut milk

1–2 teaspoons sugar, to taste

a pinch of sea salt

a packet of short wooden or bamboo skewers, soaked in water before use

SERVES 4

pork kofta kabobs
with sweet and sour sauce

These Asian-style meatball kabobs are a delicious departure from the usual grilled fare. They are best served with a hot, spicy dipping sauce and noodles. The sweet hoisin sauce is widely available in larger supermarkets and Asian markets.

To make the sauce, heat the oil in a small wok or heavy-based skillet. Stir in the garlic and chile and, when they begin to color, add the peanuts. Stir for a few minutes until the natural oil from the peanuts begins to weep. Add all the remaining ingredients (except the sugar and salt) along with ½ cup water. Let the mixture bubble up for 1 minute. Adjust the sweetness and seasoning to taste with sugar and some salt and set aside.

To make the meatballs, heat the oil in a wok or a heavy-based skillet. Add the shallots and garlic—when they begin to brown, turn off the heat and leave to cool. Put the minced pork into a bowl, tip in the stir-fried shallot and garlic, fish sauce, five-spice powder, and sugar, and season with a little salt and lots of pepper. Using your hands, knead the mixture so it is well combined. Cover and chill in the refrigerator for 2–3 hours. Knead the mixture again then tip in the breadcrumbs. Knead well to bind. Divide the mixture into roughly 20 portions and roll into balls. Thread them onto the prepared skewers. Preheat the grill and cook the kabobs for 3–4 minutes on each side, turning them from time to time, until browned.

Reheat the sauce. Serve the kofta with noodles and the hot sweet and sour sauce on the side for dipping.

Although pork should not be served rare it is quite easy to overcook it, leaving the meat dry and tough. A good test is to pierce the meat with a skewer, leave it there for a second, remove it and carefully feel how hot it is—it should feel warm, not too hot or too cold, for the perfect result.

sage-rubbed pork chops

2 tablespoons chopped
fresh sage

2 tablespoons whole-grain
mustard

2 tablespoons extra virgin
olive oil

4 large pork chops

sea salt and freshly ground
black pepper

1 recipe Fresh Tomato Salsa
(page 19), to serve

SERVES 4

Put the sage, mustard, and olive oil into a bowl and mix well. Season with a little salt and pepper, then spread the mixture all over the chops. Let marinate in the refrigerator for 1 hour.

Preheat the grill, then cook the chops over hot coals for 2½–3 minutes on each side until browned and cooked through. Serve hot with the fresh tomato salsa.

2 garlic cloves, crushed

2 tablespoons sea salt

2 tablespoons ground cumin

1 teaspoon Tabasco sauce

1 teaspoon dried oregano

½ cup honey

¼ cup sherry vinegar

⅓ cup olive oil

2 lb. barbecue pork spareribs

Salsa

2 corn cobs, husks removed, brushed with corn oil

2 red bell peppers, quartered and seeded

2 long red chile peppers, such as New Mexico, halved and seeded

4 ripe red tomatoes, halved, seeded, and finely diced

1 red onion, chopped

2 garlic cloves, crushed

2 tablespoons chopped or torn fresh cilantro

Dressing

½ teaspoon sugar

1 tablespoon corn oil

freshly squeezed juice of 1 lime

1 teaspoon salt, or to taste

freshly cracked black pepper

SERVES 4

barbecue spareribs
with Mexican salsa

The Mexican habit of grilling salsa ingredients first gives them a delicious, smoky, barbecue flavor. Toasted corn, chiles, peppers, and even tomatoes all benefit from a bit of fire! Delicious served with the sweet ribs.

To make a marinade for the spareribs, put the garlic, salt, cumin, Tabasco, oregano, honey, vinegar, and olive oil into a shallow dish and mix. Pat the ribs dry with paper towels, add them to the dish, then rub in the marinade. Cover and chill overnight.

Put the corn, pepper quarters, and chile halves onto a preheated outdoor grill or under the broiler. Toast until the pepper and chile skins and the corn are all lightly charred. Cool, then pull off the pepper and chile skins (leaving a few charred bits behind) and slice the kernels off the corn cob. Put into a bowl, add the tomatoes, onion, and garlic, then toss well.

To make the dressing for the salsa, put the sugar, corn oil, lime juice, salt, and pepper into a bowl or pitcher, mix well, then pour over the vegetables and toss again. Cover and chill for at least 30 minutes. Before serving, stir through the chopped or torn cilantro. Taste and add extra salt and freshly cracked black pepper if necessary.

When ready to cook, preheat the grill to medium, then add the ribs and cook on both sides for about 30 minutes until done. Baste from time to time with the marinade.

Cut the ribs into slices, each side of the bones, and arrange on 4 serving plates. Serve with the salsa beside or in a separate bowl. Have lots of napkins for mopping up, plus lots of cold beer.

Tex-Mex pork rack

2 racks barbecue pork spareribs, 1 lb. each

1 recipe Chile Cornbread (page 212), to serve

Marinade

2 garlic cloves, crushed

2 tablespoons sea salt

2 tablespoons ground cumin

2 teaspoons chili powder

1 teaspoon dried oregano

½ cup maple syrup or honey

¼ cup red wine vinegar

¼ cup olive oil

SERVES 4–6

Tex-Mex is a fusion of Mexican and Texan cuisines. It traditionally includes a lot of meat spiced up with hot ingredients such as chile, and has even imported spices from other cuisines, such as cumin from Indian cooking, which is included here.

Wash the ribs and pat them dry with paper towels. Transfer to a shallow, non-metal dish.

Put all the marinade ingredients into a bowl, mix well, pour over the ribs, then work in well with your hands. Cover and let marinate overnight in the refrigerator.

The next day, return the ribs to room temperature for 1 hour, then cook on a preheated medium-hot grill for about 30 minutes, turning and basting frequently with the marinade juices. Cool a little, then serve with chile cornbread.

poultry dishes

1½ lb. skinless, boneless chicken breasts, ground

2 garlic cloves, crushed

1 tablespoon chopped fresh rosemary

freshly grated zest and juice of 1 unwaxed lemon

1 egg yolk

⅓ cup dried breadcrumbs or matzo meal

1 medium eggplant

2 zucchini

4 slices focaccia

radicchio or arugula leaves

sea salt and freshly ground black pepper

olive oil, for brushing

Tapenade

⅔ cup black olives, pitted

2 anchovies in oil, drained

1 garlic clove, crushed

2 tablespoons capers, rinsed

1 teaspoon Dijon mustard

¼ cup extra virgin olive oil

freshly ground black pepper

SERVES 4

open chicken burger
with grilled vegetables

This open-faced sandwich is full of the flavors of Mediterranean cooking, with char-grilled vegetables, focaccia bread, and salty olive tapenade.

To make the tapenade, put the olives, anchovies, garlic, capers, mustard, and oil in a food processor and blend to form a fairly smooth paste. Season to taste with pepper. Transfer to a dish, cover, and store in the refrigerator for up to 5 days.

Put the chicken, garlic, rosemary, lemon zest and juice, egg yolk, breadcrumbs, and some salt and pepper in a food processor and pulse until a smooth consistency. Transfer the mixture to a bowl, cover, and chill for 30 minutes. Divide the mixture into 4 portions and shape into patties.

Cut the eggplant into 12 slices and the zucchini into 12 thin strips. Brush with olive oil and season with salt and pepper. Grill or broil the vegetables for 2–3 minutes on each side until charred and softened. Keep them warm.

Meanwhile, brush the chicken patties lightly with olive oil and grill for 5 minutes on each side until lightly charred and cooked through. Keep them warm.

Toast the focaccia and top each slice with radicchio or arugula leaves, patties, grilled vegetables, and some tapenade. Serve hot.

chicken steak burger
with Caesar dressing

4 small, skinless, boneless chicken breasts

4 slices smoked back bacon

8 slices sourdough bread

1 romaine lettuce heart, leaves separated

1 oz. Parmesan cheese, pared into shavings

sea salt and freshly ground black pepper

olive oil, for brushing

Caesar dressing

¼ cup Mayonnaise (page 199)

4 anchovies in oil, drained and finely chopped

1 garlic clove, crushed

1 teaspoon Worcestershire sauce

1 teaspoon white wine vinegar

½ teaspoon Dijon mustard

SERVES 4

The Caesar salad is as much an American icon as the burger and here the two combine perfectly in a great sourdough sandwich. You can add a poached egg to the filling, if you like.

Lay the chicken breast fillets flat on a chopping board and, using a sharp knife, cut horizontally through the thickest part but don't cut all the way through. Open the fillets out flat. Brush with olive oil and season with salt and pepper.

Preheat a grill and cook the chicken fillets for 3–4 minutes on each side until cooked through. Keep them warm. Cook the bacon on the grill for 2–3 minutes until cooked to your liking. Keep it warm. Toast the sourdough over the coals until lightly charred.

Meanwhile, to make the dressing, put the mayonnaise, anchovies, garlic, Worcestershire sauce, vinegar, and mustard in a bowl and beat well. Add salt and pepper to taste.

Spread each slice of sourdough with a little Caesar dressing and top half of them with lettuce, chicken, bacon, and Parmesan shavings. Finish with a second slice of sourdough and serve hot.

"Panini" is the Italian word for little sandwiches, usually toasted. Instead of bread, this recipe uses a chicken breast fillet, stuffed with basil and mozzarella and grilled until melted, gooey, and delicious!

chicken "panini"
with mozzarella and salsa rossa

8 oz. mozzarella cheese, cut into 8 thick slices

4 large, skinless, boneless chicken breasts

8 large basil leaves, plus extra to serve

2 garlic cloves, sliced thinly

1 tablespoon extra virgin olive oil

sea salt and freshly ground black pepper

1 recipe Salsa Rossa (see page 151), to serve

SERVES 4

Put the chicken breasts onto a board and, using a sharp knife, cut horizontally through the thickness without cutting all the way through. Open out flat and season the insides with a little salt and pepper. Put 2 basil leaves, a few garlic slices, and 2 slices of cheese into each breast, then fold back over, pressing firmly together. Secure with toothpicks.

Brush the parcels with a little oil and cook on a preheated grill or stove-top grill pan for about 8 minutes on each side until the cheese is beginning to ooze at the sides. Serve hot with the salsa rossa and sprinkle with a few basil leaves.

whole chicken roasted on the grill

3 lb. whole chicken

1 lemon, halved

4 garlic cloves, peeled

a small bunch of fresh thyme

extra virgin olive oil

sea salt and freshly ground black pepper

a grill with a lid

SERVES 4–6

Cooking with the lid on your grill creates the same effect as cooking in a conventional oven. If you don't have a grill with a lid, you can cut the chicken in half and cook on the grill for about 15 minutes on each side.

Wash the chicken thoroughly under cold running water and pat dry with paper towels.

Rub the chicken all over with the halved lemon, then put the lemon halves inside the body cavity with the garlic, cloves, and thyme. Rub a little olive oil into the skin and season liberally with salt and pepper.

Preheat the grill and when the coals are ready, rake them into two piles and carefully place a drip tray in the middle. Remove the grill rack and brush or spray it with oil. Return it to the grill and put the chicken on the rack above the drip tray. Cover with the lid, then cook over medium hot coals for 1 hour or until the skin is golden, the flesh is cooked through, and the juices run clear when the thickest part of the meat is pierced with a skewer. If any bloody juices appear, cook for a little longer.

Let the chicken rest for 10 minutes before serving.

barbecued Mexican-style Cornish hens

Butterflied Cornish hens are ideally suited to grilling, as the process of opening them out flat ensures quick and even cooking. The marinade ingredients have a Mexican flavor and work particularly well accompanied by the Creamy Corn Salsa on page 23.

4 Cornish game hens

1 recipe Creamy Corn Salsa (page 23), to serve

Mexican marinade

4 jalapeño chile peppers

8 garlic cloves, peeled

4 tablespoons freshly squeezed orange juice

2 tablespoons freshly squeezed lime juice

1 tablespoon ground cumin

1 tablespoon dried oregano or thyme

2 teaspoons sea salt

⅓ cup olive oil

1 tablespoon maple syrup or clear honey

8 wooden or bamboo skewers, soaked in water before use

SERVES 4

To butterfly the hens, turn them breast side down and, using poultry shears or sturdy scissors, cut down each side of the backbone and discard it. Turn the birds over and open them out flat, pressing down hard on the breastbone. Thread 2 skewers diagonally through each hen from the wings to the thigh bones.

To make the marinade, skewer the chiles and garlic together and cook on a preheated medium-hot grill or under a broiler for 10 minutes, turning frequently, until evenly browned. Scrape off and discard the skins from the chiles and chop the flesh coarsely. Put the flesh and seeds into a food processor, add the garlic and all the remaining marinade ingredients, and blend to a purée.

Pour the marinade over the hens and let marinate in the refrigerator overnight. Return them to room temperature for 1 hour before cooking

When ready to cook, remove the birds from their marinade and grill over medium-hot preheated coals for 12 minutes on each side, basting occasionally. Remove from the heat, let rest for 5 minutes, then serve with the creamy corn salsa.

jerk chicken wings
with avocado salsa

12 chicken wings

2 tablespoons extra virgin olive oil

1 tablespoon jerk seasoning powder or 2 tablespoons paste

freshly squeezed juice of ½ lemon

1 teaspoon sea salt

Avocado salsa

1 large ripe avocado

2 ripe tomatoes, peeled, seeded, and chopped

1 garlic clove, crushed

1 small red chile pepper, seeded and chopped

freshly squeezed juice of ½ lemon

2 tablespoons chopped fresh cilantro

1 tablespoon extra virgin olive oil

sea salt and freshly ground black pepper

SERVES 4

Jerk seasoning is Jamaica's popular spice mix, used to spark up meat, poultry, and fish. It is a combination of allspice, cinnamon, chile, nutmeg, thyme, and sugar and is widely available in powder or paste form from larger supermarkets and specialist food stores.

Put the chicken wings in a ceramic dish. Mix the oil, jerk seasoning, lemon juice, and salt in a bowl, pour over the wings, and stir well until evenly coated. Cover and let marinate overnight in the refrigerator.

The next day, cook the wings on the grill for 5–6 minutes each side, basting them occasionally with any remaining marinade until they are charred and tender.

Meanwhile, to make the salsa, put all the ingredients into a bowl, mix well, and season to taste. Serve the wings with the salsa.

Note If you don't have any jerk seasoning to hand, try another spice mix or spice paste instead. Just remember, jerk is very fiery indeed, so you need a spicy one.

char-grilled chicken breast
with mixed leaves and balsamic dressing

4 fresh boneless chicken breasts, about 2 lb.

5 oz. mixed salad leaves, such as arugula, watercress, radicchio, lambs' lettuce, or baby spinach, to serve

1 recipe Sesame Sweet Potato Packets (see page 188), to serve

Marinade

2 teaspoons Chinese five-spice powder

1 teaspoon ground ginger

2 tablespoons balsamic vinegar

1 tablespoon extra virgin olive oil

1 teaspoon sea salt

freshly ground black pepper

Balsamic dressing

4 tablespoons extra virgin olive oil

2 tablespoons balsamic vinegar

1 teaspoon mustard powder

1 tablespoon freshly squeezed lemon juice

2 teaspoons sugar

sea salt and freshly ground black pepper

a ridged stove-top grill pan

SERVES 4

The chicken in this recipe is marinaded in Chinese five-spice powder. It is distinctive and aromatic, without being overpowering, and it lends itself to marinades of all kinds.

Lay a piece of plastic wrap on a chopping board, put a chicken breast in the middle, and flatten it with the palms of your hands. Cover it with a second piece of plastic wrap, beat it flat with a meat cleaver, then remove the plastic wrap. Repeat with the remaining chicken breasts.

To make the marinade, put the five-spice powder, ginger, vinegar, olive oil, and salt in a small bowl, season with black pepper, and mix well. Spoon this over both sides of the chicken breasts, piling them on a plate as you go. Cover and leave to stand for 1–24 hours to suit. (If marinating for more than 1 hour, put the chicken in the refrigerator.)

To make the balsamic dressing, put the olive oil, vinegar, mustard powder, lemon juice, and sugar in a jar, then add salt and pepper to taste, put the lid on, and shake well.

When ready to cook, put the chicken on a preheated hot ridged stove-top grill pan on top of a preheated hot grill and cook on both sides until charred, about 10 minutes in total, lifting the corners from time to time to check that it is not burning. To make sure the chicken is cooked, cut into the thickest part with a sharp knife—if it is still pink, cook for a few more minutes.

Cover a large serving platter with the salad leaves. Arrange the cooked chicken breasts on top and drizzle the dressing over the chicken and the salad. Serve immediately with sesame sweet potato packets.

This delicious concoction of olives, lemons, fresh marjoram, and succulent chicken makes an ideal entrée for a casual backyard grill. Serve with a selection of salads, such as tomato and basil.

olive-infused chicken
with charred lemons

3 lb. whole chicken

3 oz. pitted black olives

4 tablespoons extra virgin olive oil

1 teaspoon sea salt

2 tablespoons chopped
fresh marjoram

freshly squeezed juice of 1 lemon
plus 2 lemons, halved

freshly ground black pepper

SERVES 4

To prepare the chicken, put it onto a board with the back facing upwards and, using kitchen shears, cut along each side of the backbone and remove it completely. Using your fingers, gently ease the skin away from the flesh, taking care not to tear the skin, then put the chicken into a large, shallow dish. Put the olives, olive oil, salt, marjoram, and lemon juice into a separate bowl and mix well, then pour over the chicken and push as many of the olives as possible up between the skin and flesh of the chicken. Let marinate in the refrigerator for 2 hours.

Preheat the grill, then cook the chicken cut side down over medium hot coals for 15 minutes. Using tongs, turn the chicken over and cook for a further 10 minutes until the skin is charred, the flesh is cooked through, and the juices run clear when the thickest part of the meat is pierced with a skewer. While the chicken is cooking, add the halved lemons to the grill and cook for about 10–15 minutes until charred and tender on all sides.

Let the chicken rest for 10 minutes before cutting into 4 pieces and serving with the lemons.

harissa chicken kabobs
with oranges and preserved lemon

16–20 chicken wings

4 oranges (blood oranges if available), cut into quarters

¼ cup confectioners' sugar

½ a preserved lemon*, finely shredded or chopped

a small bunch of fresh cilantro, chopped

Marinade

4 tablespoons harissa paste

2 tablespoons olive oil

sea salt

4 long, thin metal skewers

SERVES 4

With a taste of North Africa, this recipe is quick and easy and best eaten with fingers. The oranges are there to suck on after an explosion of fire on the tongue. They can be cooked separately, or threaded alternately on metal skewers.

Mix the harissa with the olive oil to form a looser paste and add a little salt. Brush the oily mixture over the chicken wings, so that they're well coated. Leave to marinate for 2 hours.

Preheat the grill. Thread the marinated chicken wings onto the skewers and cook on both sides for about 5 minutes. Once the wings begin to cook, dip the orange quarters lightly in confectioners' sugar, thread them onto skewers, and grill them for a few minutes, checking that they are slightly charred but not burnt.

Serve the chicken wings and oranges together and scatter the preserved lemon and cilantro over the top.

*Note Preserved lemons are used extensively in North African cooking and are whole lemons packed in jars with salt. The interesting thing is that you eat only the rind, which contains the essential flavor of the lemon. They are available from supermarkets and online retailers.

1 lb. skinless, boneless
chicken breasts

Marinade

1 cup plain yogurt

2 tablespoons extra virgin olive oil

2 garlic cloves, crushed

grated zest and freshly squeezed
juice of 1 unwaxed lemon

1–2 teaspoons chili powder

1 tablespoon chopped
fresh cilantro

sea salt and freshly ground
black pepper

*a packet of wooden or
bamboo skewers, soaked
in water before use*

SERVES 4

**Yogurt crusted chicken threaded onto skewers makes
ideal finger food for casual cook-outs. The yogurt tenderizes
the chicken and helps the lemon soak into the meat—and
becomes slightly crunchy when cooked over coals.**

chicken lemon skewers

Cut the chicken fillets lengthwise into ⅛-inch thick strips and
put into a shallow ceramic dish.

Put all the marinade ingredients into a bowl, stir well, and pour
over the chicken. Turn to coat, cover, and let marinate in the
refrigerator overnight.

The next day, thread the chicken onto the prepared skewers,
zigzagging the meat back and forth as you go.

Cook on a preheated grill for 3–4 minutes on each side until
charred and tender. Let cool slightly before serving.

chicken tandoori kabobs

2¼ lb. skinless, boneless chicken breasts, cut into bite-sized pieces

2 tablespoons ghee or butter, melted

Marinade

3 fresh red or green chile peppers, seeded and chopped

2–3 garlic cloves, chopped

1 oz. fresh ginger, peeled and chopped

2 tablespoons heavy cream

3 tablespoons vegetable oil

1 tablespoon paprika

2 teaspoons ground cumin

2 teaspoons ground cardamom

1 teaspoon ground cloves

1 teaspoon sea salt

To serve

crispy poppadoms

tomato and cucumber salad

limes wedges (optional)

4–6 long, thin metal skewers

SERVES 4–6

As the name of this dish denotes, it should be cooked in a tandoori oven but, as most of us don't have such a wonderful invention at home, a charcoal grill is a great substitute. Some Indian and African cooks add red food dye to the marinade to obtain the reddish coloring associated with tandoori dishes.

To prepare the marinade, use a mortar and pestle, or a food processor, to mince the chiles, garlic, and ginger to a paste. Beat in the cream and oil with 3–4 tablespoons water to form a smooth mixture. Beat in the dried spices.

Place the chicken pieces in a bowl and rub with the marinade until thoroughly coated. Cover and chill in the refrigerator for about 48 hours. Lift the chicken pieces out of the marinade and thread them onto the skewers. Prepare the grill. Brush the chicken with the melted ghee and grill for 3–4 minutes on each side. Serve with crispy poppadoms, a salad of finely diced tomato, cucumber, and onion with fresh cilantro, and wedges of lime for squeezing, if liked.

spicy chicken kabobs
with ground almonds

1 lb. 9 oz. skinless, boneless chicken breasts, cut into bite-sized pieces

freshly squeezed juice of 1 lemon

1 teaspoon sea salt

1–2 tablespoons peanut or safflower oil

1 onion, halved and sliced

1 oz. fresh ginger, peeled and finely grated

2 garlic cloves, crushed

2–3 tablespoons ground almonds

1–2 teaspoons garam masala

½ cup heavy cream

To serve

1–2 tablespoons butter

2–3 tablespoons blanched, slivered almonds

a small bunch of fresh flatleaf parsley, finely chopped

warmed flatbreads

4 long, thin metal skewers

SERVES 4

In India, Turkey, and North Africa, nuts are often used in recipes. Sometimes they are hidden in the minced meat of a kofta (meatball), or they form a coating on the meat. In this dish, the combination of almonds and browned onions in the marinade gives the meat a sweet, rich flavor.

First, toss the chicken pieces in the lemon juice and salt to blanch them. Put aside for 15 minutes.

Meanwhile, heat the oil in a skillet. Add the onion and cook until golden brown and crisp. Remove the onion from the oil and spread it out on a paper towel to drain and cool. Reserve the onion-flavored oil in the skillet.

Using a mortar and pestle or a food processor, pound the onions to a paste and beat in the ginger and garlic. Add the almonds and garam masala and bind with the cream. Tip the almond and onion mixture over the chicken and mix well. Cover and leave in the refrigerator to marinate for about 6 hours.

Thread the chicken onto the skewers and brush them with the reserved onion oil. Prepare a charcoal grill. Cook the kabobs for 3–4 minutes on each side, until the chicken is nicely browned. Quickly melt the butter in a pan and stir in the slivered almonds until golden. Toss in the parsley and spoon the mixture over the grilled chicken. Serve hot with warmed flatbreads, if liked.

1 lb. skinless, boneless chicken breasts

2 tablespoons extra virgin olive oil

freshly squeezed juice of 1 large lemon

1 tablespoon chopped fresh thyme leaves

2 garlic cloves, crushed

1 teaspoon ground turmeric

1 teaspoon ground cinnamon

½ teaspoon ground allspice

½ teaspoon salt

¼ teaspoon ground cayenne pepper

lemon wedges, to serve

plain yogurt, to serve

8 wooden or bamboo skewers, soaked in water before use

SERVES 4

chicken kabobs Moroccan-style

These delicious kabobs are wondrously flavored with scented North African spices. Serve them as snacks with a yogurt dip and flatbread, or with traditional Moroccan couscous as an entrée.

Cut the chicken lengthways into ⅛-inch strips and put into a shallow, ceramic dish. Put the oil, lemon juice, thyme, garlic, turmeric, cinnamon, allspice, salt, and cayenne into a pitcher, mix well, then pour over the chicken. Cover and marinate overnight in the refrigerator.

The next day, return to room temperature for 1 hour. Thread the strips onto skewers, zigzagging back and forth. Cook on a preheated grill for 3–4 minutes on each side until charred and cooked through. Serve with lemon wedges and yogurt.

1 lb. 9 oz. duck breasts or boned thighs, sliced into thin, bite-sized strips

1–2 tablespoons peanut or coconut oil, for brushing

1 small pineapple, peeled, cored, and sliced

Chinese plum sauce, to serve

Marinade

2–3 tablespoons light soy sauce

freshly squeezed juice of 1 lime

1–2 teaspoons sugar

1–2 garlic cloves, crushed

1 oz. fresh ginger, peeled and grated

1 small onion, grated

1–2 teaspoons ground coriander

1 teaspoon sea salt

a packet of wooden or bamboo skewers, soaked in water before use

SERVES 4

duck satay with grilled
pineapple and plum sauce

Chicken satays are popular throughout Southeast Asia but in Vietnam, Cambodia, and China, duck satays are common too. Duck is often served in the Chinese tradition of sweet and sour with a fruity sauce. You can buy prepared bottled plum sauce in Chinese grocers and most supermarkets.

To make the marinade, put the soy sauce and lime juice in a bowl with the sugar and mix until it dissolves. Add the garlic, ginger, and grated onion and stir in the ground coriander and salt.

Place the strips of duck in a bowl and pour over the marinade. Toss well, cover, and chill in the refrigerator for at least 4 hours. Thread the duck strips onto the skewers and brush them with oil.

Prepare the grill. Cook the satays for 3–4 minutes on each side, until the duck is nicely browned. Grill the slices of pineapple at the same time. When browned, cut them into bite-sized pieces and serve with the duck. Drizzle with the plum sauce to serve.

duck yakitori

⅓ cup Japanese soy sauce

3 tablespoons sake

2 tablespoons sugar

4 small duck breast fillets, about 5 oz. each, skinned

soba noodles, cooked according to the package instructions, then drained and chilled, to serve

Cucumber salad

2 tablespoons rice vinegar

2 tablespoons sugar

½ cucumber, about 8 inches, finely sliced

1 red chile pepper, seeded and chopped

8 wooden or bamboo skewers, soaked in water before use

SERVES 4

Yakitori is a Japanese-style kabob, which is usually cooked over coals and so is perfect for grills. The rich sauce in this recipe copes perfectly with the gamey taste of duck and tenderizes the flesh beautifully.

Put the soy sauce, sake, and sugar into a small saucepan and heat gently to dissolve the sugar. Cool completely.

Cut the duck lengthways into ⅛-inch strips and put into a shallow ceramic dish. Pour over the soy sauce mixture and marinate in the refrigerator for 2–4 hours or overnight.

Just before cooking the duck, prepare the salad. Put the vinegar, sugar, and 2 tablespoons water into a small saucepan, heat to dissolve the sugar, then let cool. Stir in the cucumber and chile and set aside.

Thread the duck strips onto skewers, zigzagging back and forth. Cook on a preheated grill for 2 minutes on each side until cooked through. Serve with chilled soba noodles and the cucumber salad.

fish & seafood

Chunks of swordfish coated in a spicy rub, then grilled on skewers and served with freshly cooked couscous, make the perfect al fresco lunch. Chicken would also work well, if you prefer.

Moroccan fish skewers with couscous

1½ lb. swordfish steak

extra virgin olive oil

½ recipe Moroccan Rub (page 16)

24 large bay leaves, soaked in cold water for 1 hour

2 lemons, cut into 24 chunks

freshly squeezed lemon juice, to serve

Couscous

10 oz. couscous

1¼ cups boiling water

2 oz. Parmesan cheese, freshly grated

4 tablespoons butter, melted

1 tablespoon chopped fresh thyme

sea salt and freshly ground black pepper

8 wooden or bamboo skewers, soaked in water before use

SERVES 4

Using a sharp knife, cut the swordfish into 32 cubes and put into a shallow ceramic dish. Add a sprinkle of olive oil and the Moroccan rub and toss well until the fish is evenly coated. Let marinate in the refrigerator for 1 hour.

About 10 minutes before cooking the fish, put the couscous into a strainer and rinse under cold running water to moisten all the grains, then put into a steamer and steam for 10 minutes or until the grains have softened. Transfer the couscous to a warmed serving dish and immediately stir in the Parmesan cheese, melted butter, thyme, and seasonings. Keep the couscous warm.

Meanwhile, preheat the grill. Thread the fish, bay leaves and chunks of lemon onto the prepared skewers and cook over hot coals for 3–4 minutes, turning halfway through, until cooked. Serve the skewers on a bed of couscous, sprinkled with olive oil and lemon juice.

Note One hour is sufficient to flavor the fish with the spice rub, any longer and the flavors of the rub can become overpowering.

2 unwaxed lemons

1 cup extra virgin olive oil

1 tablespoon dried oregano

2 garlic cloves, finely chopped

2 tablespoons chopped fresh
flatleaf parsley

6 bream or snapper, about 12 oz.
each, well cleaned and scaled

sea salt and freshly ground
black pepper

SERVES 6

char-grilled fish
bathed in oregano and lemon

**This recipe for the classic summer dish of char-grilled
fish with lemon, oregano, and garlic, uses bream, but you
could use other small fish such as snapper, red mullet, or
even trout if you prefer.**

Grate the zest of 1 lemon into a small bowl and squeeze in the
juice. Add ¾ cup of the oil, the oregano, garlic, parsley, salt, and
pepper. Leave to infuse for at least 1 hour.

Wash and dry the fish inside and out. Using a sharp knife,
cut several slashes into each side. Squeeze the juice from the
remaining lemon into a bowl, add the remaining ¼ cup of oil,
salt, and pepper, and rub the mixture all over the fish.

Heat the flat plate of an outdoor grill for 10 minutes, add the fish,
and cook for 3–4 minutes on each side until charred and cooked
through. Alternatively, use a large, heavy-based skillet or stove-top
grill pan. Transfer to a large, warm platter, pour over the lemon
dressing, and let rest for 5 minutes before serving.

red snapper
with parsley salad

4 red snapper, cleaned and well scaled, about 8 oz. each

1 recipe Herb, Lemon, and Garlic Marinade (page 15)

Parsley salad

⅓ cup raisins

2 tablespoons verjuice* or white grape juice

leaves from a large bunch of fresh parsley

¼ cup pine nuts, toasted

2 oz. feta cheese, crumbled

3 tablespoons extra virgin olive oil

2 teaspoons balsamic vinegar

sea salt and freshly ground black pepper

SERVES 4

Even if the snapper has already been scaled by the fishmonger, go over it again to remove any stray scales, they are huge! A fish grilling basket could also be useful for cooking this fish.

Using a sharp knife, cut several slashes into each side of the fish. Put into a shallow ceramic dish and add the marinade. Let marinate in the refrigerator for 4 hours, but return to room temperature for 1 hour before cooking.

Just before cooking the fish, make the salad. Put the raisins into a bowl, add the verjuice, and let soak for 15 minutes. Drain and set the liquid aside. Put the parsley, pine nuts, soaked raisins, and feta into a bowl. Put the olive oil, vinegar, and reserved raisin liquid into a separate bowl and mix well. Pour over the salad and toss until the leaves are well coated. Season with salt and pepper.

Preheat the grill, then cook the fish over hot coals for 4–5 minutes on each side, let rest briefly, and serve with the salad.

*Note Verjuice, which is used in the salad dressing, is produced from the juice of unripe grapes. It is available from Italian gourmet stores. If you can't find it, use white grape juice instead.

1 heaping teaspoon fennel seeds

1 heaping teaspoon dried oregano

1 teaspoon cumin seeds

1 teaspoon sea salt

1 teaspoon green or black peppercorns

¼ teaspoon dried hot red pepper flakes

6 small seabass, gutted and scaled (ask the fishmonger or assistant at the fish counter to do this for you)

extra virgin olive oil spray

3 unwaxed lemons

a few bay leaves

4 baby fennel bulbs

12 oz. cherry tomatoes

wedges of lemon, to serve

6 wooden or bamboo skewers, soaked in water before use

SERVES 6

Sicilian-spiced seabass with grilled tomatoes and baby fennel

A simple but impressive dish that is easy to cook on the grill. If whole fish don't appeal, you could make this recipe with tuna or swordfish steaks.

Heat a gas grill or light a charcoal grill.

Crush the fennel seeds, oregano, cumin seeds, salt, peppercorns, and chile together thoroughly in a mortar with a pestle. Make 3 slashes in each side of the fish with a sharp knife. Spray the fish with olive oil and rub the pounded spices over the fish and into the slits. Cut 2 of the lemons in half vertically, then cut 1½ into thin slices. Cut or tear the bay leaves into halves or thirds. Place half a slice of lemon and a piece of bay leaf in each slit.

Cut each fennel bulb in quarters lengthwise and thread the cherry tomatoes onto the skewers. Spray the fish, fennel, and tomatoes with oil and grill over medium heat until charred, turning them halfway through, removing them as they are cooked. Serve with wedges of lemon.

grilled salmon steaks
with basil and parmesan butter

Flavored butters help to keep the fish deliciously moist, but be sure to watch the steaks carefully while cooking as they can easily overcook. Brushing the bars of the grill with a little oil will prevent the salmon from sticking.

6 fresh salmon steaks, cut about 1 inch thick, 3 lb. total weight

Basil and Parmesan butter

1½ sticks unsalted butter

¼ cup freshly grated Parmesan cheese

1 teaspoon balsamic or sherry vinegar

¾ cup fresh basil leaves, sliced

freshly ground black pepper

Marinade

1 large garlic clove, crushed

⅔ cup light olive oil

2 tablespoons balsamic or sherry vinegar

1–2 sprigs of fresh thyme, crushed

SERVES 6

To make the basil and Parmesan butter, beat the butter until soft. Gradually beat in the grated Parmesan, vinegar, basil, and ground black pepper to taste. Scoop onto a piece of wet waxed paper and roll into a cylinder. Wrap in plastic wrap and refrigerate (or freeze) for at least 1 hour, or until firm.

Put the marinade ingredients in a wide, shallow dish, mix well, then add the salmon steaks and turn to coat well. Cover and let marinate for 20–30 minutes. Lift the steaks from the marinade and pat dry with paper towels.

Heat an outdoor grill until the coals are medium hot and white (no longer red). Lightly oil the grill bars, add the salmon, and cook for about 3 minutes on each side until crisp and brown on the outside and just opaque all the way through—overcooked salmon is dry, so be careful to cook it properly. Serve the salmon steaks covered with slices of the chilled butter melting on top.

Note If using other herbs, such as parsley, tarragon, or marjoram, always use fresh: dried herbs are not very successful.

2 fresh tail-end salmon fillets, 14 oz. each, skin on

sea salt and freshly ground black pepper

Mustard marinade

3 tablespoons Dijon mustard

2 tablespoons soy sauce

1 large garlic clove, crushed

1 tablespoon chopped fresh ginger

3 tablespoons chopped fresh tarragon

thick kitchen twine, soaked in cold water before use

SERVES 6–8

mustard-grilled salmon tail

A fantastic way to roast or grill a gigot of salmon. If you have a grill with a lid, the salmon will take a shorter time to cook—just don't keep lifting the lid.

To make the marinade, mix the mustard, soy, garlic, ginger, and tarragon in a bowl.

Put one salmon fillet skin-side down on a board and spread liberally with the mustard mix. Season well. Arrange the other fillet on top and tie up in 3 or 4 places with twine. Cover and refrigerate for about 2 hours for the flavors to permeate the flesh. Return to room temperature before cooking.

When ready to cook, preheat an outdoor grill until the coals are white and no longer red. Brush the salmon with a little oil and grill over medium hot coals for about 15 minutes per side, or until the fish is opaque all the way through.

Serve immediately by untying the twine and lifting off the top fillet. Lift the salmon off the skin to serve.

Note There are heavy foil trays available: if you "roast" the salmon on one of these, it will catch the delicious juices.

A great way to prepare whole salmon is to remove the central bone from the fish, then tie the two fillets back together. If your filleting skills are limited, just ask your friendly fishmonger to fillet the whole fish for you.

whole salmon stuffed with herbs

4 lb. whole salmon, filleted

1 stick butter, softened

1 cup chopped, fresh soft-leaf mixed herbs, such as basil, chives, mint, parsley, and tarragon

grated zest of 1 unwaxed lemon

1 garlic clove, crushed

sea salt and freshly ground black pepper

olive oil, for brushing

kitchen twine

SERVES 8

Put the salmon fillets flat onto a board, flesh side up. Carefully pull out any remaining bones with tweezers.

Put the butter, herbs, lemon zest, garlic, and plenty of pepper into a small bowl and beat well. Spread the mixture over one of the salmon fillets and put the second on the top, arranging them top to tail.

Using kitchen twine, tie the fish together at 1-inch intervals. Brush with a little oil, sprinkle with salt and freshly ground black pepper, and cook on the flat plate of a grill for 10 minutes on each side. Let rest for a further 10 minutes. Remove the string and serve the fish cut into portions.

stuffed char-grilled sardines

4 good-sized fresh sardines

2 tablespoons olive oil

4–6 scallions, finely sliced

2–3 garlic cloves, crushed

1 teaspoon cumin seeds, crushed

1 teaspoon ground sumac
(see note on page 147)

1 tablespoon pine nuts

1 tablespoon currants, soaked
in warm water for 15 minutes
and drained

a small bunch of fresh flatleaf
parsley, finely chopped

sea salt and freshly ground
black pepper

Basting

3 tablespoons olive oil

freshly squeezed juice of 1 lemon

1–2 teaspoons ground sumac

*a packet of wooden or bamboo
skewers, soaked in water
before use*

SERVES 4

This dish is best made with good-sized plump, fresh sardines, which are slit from head to tail with the back bone removed. Full of Mediterranean flavors, this is a great recipe for outdoor cooking on the grill while enjoying the summer sunshine.

To prepare the sardines, remove the bone, gently massage the area around it to loosen it. Using your fingers, carefully prise out the bone, snapping it off at each end, while keeping the fish intact. Rinse the fish and pat it dry before stuffing.

Heat the oil in a heavy-based pan and stir in the scallions until soft. Add the garlic, cumin, and sumac. Stir in the pine nuts and pre-soaked currants, and sauté until the pine nuts begin to turn golden. Toss in the parsley and season with salt and pepper. Leave to cool.

Place the sardines on a flat surface and spread the filling inside each one. When stuffed, seal the fish by threading the skewers through the soft belly flaps.

Mix together the olive oil, lemon juice, and sumac and brush some of it over the sardines. Prepare a charcoal grill. Cook the stuffed fish for 2–3 minutes on each side, basting them with the rest of the olive oil mixture. Serve immediately.

swordfish kabobs
with oranges and sumac

1 lb. 2 oz. boned swordfish, cut into bite-sized chunks

2 oranges, cut into wedges

a handful of fresh bay leaves

2–3 teaspoons ground sumac*

Marinade

1 onion, grated

1–2 garlic cloves, crushed

freshly squeezed juice of ½ a lemon

2–3 tablespoons olive oil

1–2 teaspoons tomato paste

sea salt and freshly ground black pepper

4 metal skewers or 4–6 wooden skewers, soaked in water before use

SERVES 4

Any firm-fleshed fish, such as tuna, trout, salmon, monkfish, and sea bass, can be used for these mighty Middle Eastern kabobs. Make life easy and buy the swordfish ready boned from the fishmonger. Exotic sumac adds a lemony tang.

In a shallow bowl, mix together the ingredients for the marinade. Toss the chunks of swordfish in the marinade and set aside to marinate for 30 minutes.

Thread the marinated fish onto the skewers, alternating it with the orange segments and the occasional bay leaf. If there is any marinade left, brush it over the kabobs.

Prepare a charcoal grill. Cook the kabobs for 2–3 minutes on each side, until the fish is nicely browned. Sprinkle the kabobs with sumac and serve.

*Note Sumac is an increasingly popular spice. It grows wild, but is also cultivated in Italy, Sicily, and throughout the Middle East. It is widely used in Lebanese, Syrian, Turkish, and Iranian cooking. The red berries have an astringent quality, with a pleasing sour-fruit flavor. They are used whole, but ground sumac is available from Middle Eastern grocers or specialist online retailers.

Swordfish is delicious char-grilled, but it is easy to overcook, and will become tough, so follow the timings below and err on the side of caution—you can always put the fish back on the grill for a moment or two longer.

seared swordfish with
new potatoes, beans, and olives

4 swordfish steaks, 8 oz. each

1 tablespoon extra virgin olive oil

1 lb. new potatoes, halved if large

8 oz. string beans, trimmed

2 oz. pitted black or green olives, chopped

balsamic vinegar, to serve

Dressing

6 tablespoons extra virgin olive oil

2 tablespoons freshly squeezed lemon juice

½ teaspoon sugar

1 tablespoon chopped fresh chives

sea salt and freshly ground black pepper

SERVES 4

Brush the swordfish steaks with the oil, season with salt and pepper, and set aside.

To make the dressing, put the oil into a bowl and add the lemon juice, sugar, chives, salt, and pepper. Beat well and set aside.

Cook the potatoes in a saucepan of lightly salted boiling water for 10 minutes, add the beans, and cook for a further 3–4 minutes or until the potatoes and beans are just tender. Drain well, add the olives and half the dressing, and toss well.

Cook the swordfish steaks on a preheated outdoor grill for about 1½ minutes on each side. Let rest in a warm oven for 5 minutes, then serve with the warm potato salad, sprinkled with the remaining dressing and a splash of balsamic vinegar.

peppered tuna steak
with salsa rossa

6 tablespoons mixed peppercorns, coarsely crushed

6 tuna steaks, 8 oz. each

1 tablespoon extra virgin olive oil, for brushing

mixed leaf salad, to serve

Salsa rossa

1 large red bell pepper

1 tablespoon extra virgin olive oil

2 garlic cloves, crushed

2 large ripe tomatoes, peeled and roughly chopped

a small pinch of dried hot red pepper flakes

1 tablespoon dried oregano

1 tablespoon red wine vinegar

sea salt and freshly ground black pepper

SERVES 6

Salsa rossa is one of those divine Italian sauces that transforms simple meat and fish dishes into food nirvana. The slight sweetness from the bell peppers is a good foil for the spicy pepper crust.

To make the salsa rossa, broil the bell pepper until charred all over, then put into a plastic bag and let cool. Remove and discard the skin and seeds, reserving any juices, then chop the flesh.

Put the oil into a skillet, heat gently, then add the garlic and sauté for 3 minutes. Add the tomatoes, hot red pepper flakes, and oregano and simmer gently for 15 minutes. Stir in the peppers and the vinegar and simmer for a further 5 minutes to evaporate any excess liquid.

Transfer to a blender and purée until fairly smooth. Add salt and pepper to taste and let cool. It may be stored in a screw-top jar in the refrigerator for up to 3 days.

Put the crushed peppercorns onto a large plate. Brush the tuna steaks with oil, then press the crushed peppercorns into the surface. Preheat the grill, add the tuna, and cook for 1 minute on each side. Wrap loosely in foil and let rest for 5 minutes before serving with the salsa rossa and a salad of mixed leaves.

Dukkah is a Middle Eastern side dish comprising mixed nuts and spices, which are ground to a coarse powder and served as a dip for warm bread. Here, it is used as a coating for grilled tuna. Preserved lemons are available from French, North African, or good gourmet food stores, and some larger supermarkets.

4 tuna steaks, about 8 oz. each

3 tablespoons sesame seeds

2 tablespoons coriander seeds

½ tablespoon cumin seeds

¼ cup blanched almonds, chopped

½ teaspoon salt

freshly ground black pepper

olive oil, for brushing

Preserved lemon salsa

1 preserved lemon

¼ cup semi-dried tomatoes

2 scallions, very finely chopped

1 tablespoon coarsely chopped fresh parsley

3 tablespoons extra virgin olive oil

¼ teaspoon sugar

SERVES 4

dukkah crusted tuna
with preserved lemon salsa

To make the salsa, chop the preserved lemon and tomatoes finely and put into a bowl. Stir in the scallions, parsley, olive oil, and sugar and set aside until ready to serve.

Wash the tuna steaks under cold running water and pat dry with paper towels.

Put the sesame seeds into a dry skillet and toast over medium heat until golden and aromatic. Remove and let cool. Repeat with the coriander seeds, cumin seeds, and almonds. Transfer to a spice grinder (or clean coffee grinder) and grind. Alternatively, use a mortar and pestle. Add the salt and a little pepper.

Preheat the grill. Brush the tuna steaks with olive oil and coat with the dukkah mixture. Cook over hot coals for 1 minute on each side, top with the salsa and serve.

2 lb. monkfish tail, cut into chunks

12–16 cherry tomatoes

1–2 teaspoons smoked paprika, to dust

1–2 lemons, cut into wedges, to serve

Chermoula

2 garlic cloves

1 teaspoon coarse sea salt

1–2 teaspoons cumin seeds, crushed or ground

1 fresh red chile pepper, seeded and chopped

freshly squeezed juice of 1 lemon

2 tablespoons olive oil

a small bunch of fresh cilantro, roughly chopped

4–6 metal skewers or 4–6 wooden skewers, soaked in water before use

SERVES 4–6

monkfish kabobs
with chermoula

Chermoula is a classic Moroccan flavoring of garlic, chile, cumin, and fresh cilantro, which is employed as a marinade for fish and chicken tagines and grilled dishes. Any meaty, white fish can be used for this recipe but monkfish cooks particularly well over charcoal.

To make the chermoula, use a mortar and pestle to pound the garlic with the salt to a smooth paste. Add the cumin, chile, lemon juice, and olive oil and stir in the cilantro.

Put the fish chunks in a shallow dish and rub with the chermoula. Cover and chill in the refrigerator for 1–2 hours.

Thread the marinated monkfish and cherry tomatoes alternately onto the skewers. Preheat the grill. Cook the kabobs for about 2 minutes on each side, until the monkfish is nicely browned. Dust with a little paprika and serve with wedges of lemon for squeezing over them.

about 30 preserved vine leaves

4–5 large, skinless fillets of white fish, with all bones removed

Marinade

2–3 garlic cloves, crushed

1–2 teaspoons ground cumin

4 tablespoons olive oil

freshly squeezed juice of 1 lemon

1 teaspoon sea salt

Tangy herb sauce

¼ cup white wine vinegar or freshly squeezed lemon juice

1–2 tablespoons sugar

a pinch of saffron threads

1 onion, finely chopped

2 garlic cloves, finely chopped

2–3 scallions, finely sliced

a thumb-sized piece of fresh ginger, peeled and grated

2 fresh hot red or green chile peppers, finely sliced

a small bunch of fresh cilantro, finely chopped

a small bunch of fresh mint, finely chopped

sea salt

a packet of short wooden or bamboo skewers, soaked in water before use

SERVES 4

vine-wrapped fish kabobs
with tangy herb sauce

For these Mediterranean kabobs, almost any kind of firm, white fish fillet will do—monkfish or haddock work well. The fish is prepared in a simple marinade and then wrapped in the vine leaves, which become crisper with cooking whilst keeping the fish moist.

First wash the vine leaves and soak them in several changes of water for 1 hour.

To prepare the marinade, mix all the ingredients together in a shallow bowl. Cut each fillet of fish into roughly 8 bite-sized pieces and coat in the marinade. Cover and chill in the refrigerator for 1 hour.

Meanwhile, prepare the tangy herb sauce. Put the vinegar in a small saucepan with the sugar and 1–2 tablespoons water. Heat until the sugar has dissolved. Bring to a boil for 1 minute, then leave to cool. Add the other ingredients, mix well, and spoon the sauce into small individual bowls.

Lay the prepared vine leaves on a flat surface and place a piece of marinated fish in the centre of each one. Fold the edges over the fish and wrap the leaf up into a small parcel. Push the parcels carefully onto the individual skewers and brush the leaves with any remaining marinade.

Preheat the grill. Cook the kabobs for 2–3 minutes on each side. Serve immediately with a dish of the tangy herb sauce on the side for dipping.

This is a great way to cook clams on the grill, where all the wonderful juices are collected in the foil parcel. Mop them up with plenty of crusty bread.

clam packages
with garlic butter

2 lb. littleneck clams

1¼ sticks unsalted butter, softened

grated zest and freshly squeezed juice of ½ unwaxed lemon

2 garlic cloves, crushed

2 tablespoons chopped fresh parsley

freshly ground black pepper

fresh crusty bread, to serve

SERVES 4

Wash the clams under cold running water and scrub the shells. Discard any with broken shells or any that refuse to close when tapped lightly with a knife. Shake the clams dry and divide between 4 pieces of foil.

Put the butter, lemon zest and juice, garlic, parsley, and pepper into a bowl and beat well. Divide equally between the clams. Wrap the foil over the clams and seal the edges to form packages.

Preheat the grill, then put the packages onto the grill rack and cook for 5 minutes. Check 1 parcel to see if the clams have opened and serve if ready or cook a little longer, if needed. Serve with crusty bread.

1 lb. 2 oz., shrimp, deveined and trimmed of heads, feelers, and legs

leaves from a small bunch of fresh cilantro, to serve

2–4 fresh green chile peppers, seeded and sliced, to serve

Marinade

3 tablespoons tamarind pulp*

2 tablespoons sweet soy sauce

1 tablespoon sugar

freshly ground black pepper

a packet of wooden or bamboo skewers, soaked in water before use

SERVES 2–4

char-grilled tamarind shrimp

This is popular street food in Malaysia and Indonesia. The aroma emanating from the stalls as the marinated shrimp are grilled over charcoal, makes you feel very hungry.

Rinse the prepared shrimp well, pat dry, and, using a very sharp knife, make an incision along the curve of the tail. Set aside.

Put the tamarind pulp in a bowl and add 1 cup of warm water. Soak the pulp, until soft, squeezing it with your fingers to help dissolve it. Strain the liquid and discard any fibre or seeds. In a bowl, mix together the tamarind juice, soy sauce, sugar, and black pepper. Pour it over the shrimp, rubbing it over the shells and into the incision in the tails. Cover, refrigerate, and leave to marinate for about 1 hour.

Preheat the grill. Insert a skewer into each marinated shrimp. Cook the shrimp for about 3 minutes on each side, until the shells have turned orange, brushing them with extra marinade as they cook. Serve immediately, garnished with the cilantro leaves and chiles.

*Note Tamarind lends a rich, sweet-sour flavor to dishes. The tropical trees produce fresh pods that are either sold fresh or processed into pulp or paste for convenience and long shelf life. Look out for it in Asian or Caribbean grocers—semi-dried tamarind pulp comes in soft rectangular blocks sealed in plastic wrap. The darker concentrated paste is sold in tubs and is a more processed product.

shrimp with chile oil and pistachio and mint pesto

Shrimp make the fastest, freshest, most impressive dish you can imagine. If you can't find uncooked shrimp, use precooked ones—just sprinkle them with the chile oil and lemon juice and serve with the cool and refreshing pesto.

24 large uncooked shrimp, shelled and deveined

4 tablespoons chile oil*

freshly squeezed juice of 1 lemon

fresh crusty bread, to serve

Pistachio and mint pesto

2 oz. shelled pistachio nuts

a bunch of fresh mint

1 garlic clove, crushed

2 scallions, chopped

½ cup extra virgin olive oil

1 tablespoon white wine vinegar

sea salt and freshly ground black pepper

a packet of wooden or bamboo skewers, soaked in water before use

SERVES 4

To make the pesto, put the pistachio nuts, mint, garlic, and scallions into a food processor and grind coarsely. Add the oil and purée until fairly smooth and green. Stir in the vinegar and season to taste. Set aside while you prepare the shrimp, or store in the refrigerator for up to 5 days.

Put the shrimp into a shallow dish and sprinkle with the chile oil, salt, and pepper. Cover and let marinate for at least 30 minutes or longer, if possible.

When ready to serve, thread the shrimp onto skewers and cook on a preheated grill for about 2 minutes on each side until charred and tender—the flesh should be just opaque. Do not overcook or the shrimp will be tough.

Arrange on separate plates or a large platter, sprinkle with fresh lemon juice, and serve with the pesto and crusty bread to mop up the juices.

*Note Olive oils infused with chile and other flavorings are widely available in most supermarkets or gourmet food stores.

char-grilled shrimp
with avocado chile salsa

3–5 uncooked shrimp per person, depending on size, with shells

2 tablespoons chile oil

freshly squeezed juice of 2 limes

a pinch of sea salt

2 tablespoons brown sugar

Avocado chile salsa

2 red onions, quartered, then finely sliced

1 red chile pepper, such as serrano, seeded and sliced or diced

finely grated zest and freshly squeezed juice of 1 unwaxed lime

2 large, ripe Hass avocados, halved, with pits removed*

2 ripe red tomatoes, halved, seeded, and diced

a large handful of fresh cilantro

sea salt and coarsely cracked black pepper

SERVES 4

Avocado is a Mexican ingredient, so it tastes good in a salsa (which is, after all, a Latin American dish). For this recipe, use the warty-skinned, greenish-purple Hass avocado, which are the most flavorsome.

To make the salsa, put the onion, chile, and half the lime juice into a bowl and set aside to marinate for a few minutes.

Using a small teaspoon or coffee spoon, scoop out small balls of avocado into a serving bowl. Add the lime zest and remaining juice and turn gently to coat.

Add the diced tomatoes to the onion mixture, toss gently, then add the avocado. Tear the cilantro leaves over the top and sprinkle with the sea salt and black pepper.

Meanwhile, slit the shrimp down the back and pull out the black vein, if any. Put the chile oil, lime juice, salt, and sugar into a bowl, add the shrimp, and toss to coat. Using your fingers, push the sauce into the slit and set aside for 30 minutes. Preheat a grill to medium hot, add the shrimp, then cook on both sides until just opaque.

Serve the shrimp with the avocado chile salsa. Flour tortillas, warmed on the grill, are also a delicious accompaniment.

*Note Always prepare avocado at the last moment and coat in a little citrus juice. Avocado turns brown very quickly—don't believe the old wives' tale that the pit prevents this.

12 large fresh shrimp, shelled to the tail

8 fresh scallops, shelled and thoroughly cleaned

8 cherry tomatoes

1 green bell pepper, cut into bite-sized squares

Marinade

freshly squeezed juice of 2 lemons

4 garlic cloves, crushed

1 teaspoon ground cumin

1 teaspoon paprika

sea salt

Walnut sauce

1 cup shelled walnut halves

2 slices day-old bread, soaked in water and squeezed dry

2–3 garlic cloves, crushed

3–4 tablespoons olive oil

freshly squeezed juice of 1 lemon

a dash of white wine vinegar

sea salt and freshly ground black pepper

a packet of wooden or bamboo skewers, soaked in water before use

SERVES 4

shrimp and scallop kabobs with walnut sauce

This is one of the most popular ways to enjoy the jumbo shrimp and scallops along the Mediterranean coast of Syria, Turkey, and Lebanon. Threaded onto skewers with bell peppers and tomatoes, they are served char-grilled with a delicious garlicky walnut sauce.

To make the marinade, mix together the lemon juice, garlic, cumin, paprika, and a little salt in a bowl. Rub the mixture into the shrimp and scallops. Cover, refrigerate, and leave to marinate for about 1 hour.

Meanwhile, prepare the walnut sauce. Using a mortar and pestle, pound the walnuts to a paste, or whizz them in a food processor. Add the bread and garlic and pound to a paste. Drizzle in the olive oil, stirring all the time, and beat in the lemon juice and vinegar. The sauce should be smooth with the consistency of heavy cream—if it's too dry, stir in a little water. Season the sauce with salt and pepper and set aside.

Thread the shrimp and scallops onto the skewers, alternating with the tomatoes and bell pepper, until all the ingredients are used up. Preheat the grill. Cook the kabobs for 2 minutes on each side, basting with any of the leftover marinade, until the shrimp shells are orange, the scallops tender, and the tomatoes and peppers lightly browned. Serve hot with the walnut sauce on the side for dipping.

skewered scallops
with coconut dressing

Seafood has a natural affinity with coconut, and it is a combination often found in Indonesian and Thai cooking. The tangy lime and chile marinade cuts wonderfully through the richness of the sweet coconut and succulent, meaty scallops.

24 large scallops, without corals

2 tablespoons peanut oil

grated zest of 2 limes

2 red chile peppers, such as serrano, seeded and chopped

2 teaspoons grated fresh ginger

1 garlic clove, crushed

1 tablespoon Thai fish sauce

Coconut milk dressing

⅓ cup coconut milk

1 tablespoon Thai fish sauce

2 teaspoons sugar

2 teaspoons coconut or rice wine vinegar*

6 wooden or bamboo skewers, soaked in water before use

SERVES 6

Trim the tough white muscle from the side of each scallop. Put the scallops into a shallow non-metal dish.

Put the peanut oil, lime zest, chiles, ginger, garlic, and fish sauce into a small pitcher or bowl, mix well, then pour over the scallops. Let marinate in the refrigerator for 1 hour.

To make the dressing, put the coconut milk, fish sauce, sugar, and vinegar into a small saucepan, heat gently to dissolve the sugar, then bring to a gentle simmer until thickened slightly. Remove from the heat and let cool completely.

Meanwhile, preheat the outdoor grill until hot.

Thread the scallops onto the prepared skewers and cook for 1 minute on each side. Don't overcook or the scallops will be tough. Serve with the coconut dressing and wedges of lime.

*Note Coconut and palm vinegar are used in Thailand and the Philippines: both are milder than regular vinegars. Buy them in Asian food stores or use white rice vinegar as an alternative.

Piri-piri, a Portuguese chile condiment traditionally used to baste grilled chicken, is a combination of chopped red chiles, olive oil, and vinegar. It is generally very hot and only a drizzle is needed to add spice to grilled food. In this recipe the heat is tempered, but you can use more chiles if you like it hotter. It works very well with squid.

squid piri-piri

8 medium squid bodies, about 8 oz. each*

freshly squeezed juice of 1 lemon, plus extra lemon wedges, to serve

sea salt

Piri-piri sauce

8 small red chile peppers

1¼ cups extra virgin olive oil

1 tablespoon white wine vinegar

sea salt and freshly ground black pepper

16 wooden or bamboo skewers, soaked in water before use

SERVES 4

To prepare the squid, put the squid body on a board and, using a sharp knife, cut down one side and open the tube out flat. Scrape away any remaining insides and wash and dry well.

Skewer each opened-out tube with 2 skewers, running them up the long sides of each piece. Rub a little sea salt over each one and squeeze over the lemon juice. Marinate in the refrigerator for 30 minutes.

Meanwhile, to make the piri-piri, finely chop the whole chiles without seeding them and transfer to a small jar or bottle. Add the oil, vinegar, and a little salt and pepper. Shake well and set aside.

Meanwhile, preheat a outdoor grill until hot.

Baste the squid with a little of the piri-piri and cook for 1–1½ minutes on each side until charred. Drizzle with extra sauce and serve with lemon wedges.

*Note If the squid includes the tentacles, cut them off in one piece, thread with a skewer, and cook and marinate in the same way as the tubes.

vegetables

2 eggplant, cut into chunks

2 zucchini, cut into chunks

2–3 bell peppers, stalks removed, seeded, and cut into chunks

12–16 cherry tomatoes

4 red onions, cut into quarters

Marinade

4 tablespoons olive oil

freshly squeezed juice of ½ lemon

2 garlic cloves, crushed

1 teaspoon sea salt

Garlicky pesto

3–4 garlic cloves, roughly chopped

leaves from a large bunch of fresh basil (at least 30–40 leaves)

½ teaspoon sea salt

2–3 tablespoons pine nuts

extra virgin olive oil, as required

¼ cup freshly grated Parmesan cheese

4–6 metal skewers or wooden skewers, soaked in water before use

SERVES 4–6

summer vegetable kabobs
with homemade garlicky pesto

Full of sunshine flavors, these kabobs can be served with couscous and a salad, or with pasta tossed in some of the pesto sauce. Homemade pesto is very personal— some people like it very garlicky, as in this recipe, others prefer lots of basil or Parmesan—so simply adjust the quantities to suit your taste.

To make the pesto, use a mortar and pestle to pound the garlic with the basil leaves and salt—the salt will act as an abrasive and help to grind. (If you only have a small mortar and pestle, you may have to do this in batches.) Add the pine nuts and pound them to a paste. Slowly drizzle in some olive oil and bind with the grated Parmesan. Continue to pound and grind with the pestle, adding in enough oil to make a smooth sauce. Set aside.

Put all the prepared vegetables in a bowl. Mix together the olive oil, lemon juice, garlic, and salt and pour it over the vegetables. Using your hands, toss the vegetables gently in the marinade, then thread them onto the skewers.

Preheat the grill. Cook the kabobs for 2–3 minutes on each side, until the vegetables are nicely browned. Serve the kabobs with the pesto on the side for drizzling.

Mushrooms, with their meaty texture and earthy flavor, provide vegetarians with a great meat-free alternative to hamburgers. Here they are served with a garlic sauce, but you can also serve them traditionally with mustard, salad, cheese, and pickles.

mushroom burgers
with caramelized garlic aïoli

8 large portobello mushrooms

4–6 tablespoons olive oil

4 large burger buns, halved

4 tablespoons Chile Relish (page 53)

a handful of arugula leaves

sea salt and freshly ground black pepper

Caramelized garlic aïoli

1 large head garlic

2 egg yolks

1 teaspoon Dijon mustard

1 teaspoon freshly squeezed lemon juice

1 cup olive oil

SERVES 4

To make the aïoli, wrap the garlic head in foil and bake in a preheated oven at 400°F for 45–50 minutes, until the garlic is really soft. Let cool, then squeeze the garlic purée out of each clove into a bowl.

Put the egg yolks, mustard, lemon juice, salt, and the garlic purée in a food processor and blend briefly until frothy. With the motor running, gradually pour in the oil through the funnel until the sauce is thickened and all the oil incorporated. Transfer the aïoli to a bowl, cover the surface with plastic wrap, and chill until required.

Peel the mushroom caps and trim the stalks so they are flat with the cups. Brush lightly with olive oil, season with salt and pepper, and grill or broil for 4–5 minutes on each side until softened and cooked through.

Toast the buns and fill with the mushrooms, caramelized garlic aïoli, chile relish, and some arugula leaves. Serve hot.

32 large fresh bay leaves

20 small beets

20 pearl onions, unpeeled

3 tablespoons extra virgin olive oil

1 tablespoon balsamic vinegar

sea salt and freshly ground black pepper

8 metal skewers

SERVES 4

For this dish, you need beets and pearl onions of roughly the same size, so they will cook evenly on the grill. Vegetable brochettes are an excellent accompaniment to grilled meats or fish, or a good vegetarian alternative.

beet and pearl onion brochettes

Put the bay leaves into a bowl, cover with cold water, and let soak for 1 hour before cooking.

Cut the stalks off the beets and wash well under cold running water. Put the beets and pearl onions into a large saucepan of lightly salted boiling water and blanch for 5 minutes. Drain and refresh under cold running water. Pat dry with paper towels, then peel the onions.

Preheat the grill. Thread the beets, onions, and damp bay leaves onto the skewers, sprinkle with the olive oil and vinegar, and season well with salt and pepper. Cook over medium hot coals for 20–25 minutes, turning occasionally, until charred and tender, then serve.

1¼ cups dried chickpeas

1 small onion, finely chopped

2 garlic cloves, crushed

½ bunch of fresh flatleaf parsley

½ bunch of fresh cilantro

2 teaspoons ground coriander

½ teaspoon baking powder

4 hero rolls

a handful of salad leaves

2 tomatoes, diced

sea salt and freshly
ground black pepper

peanut or safflower oil,
for shallow frying

Tahini yogurt sauce

½ cup thick plain yogurt

1 tablespoon tahini paste

1 garlic clove, crushed

½ tablespoon freshly squeezed
lemon juice

1 tablespoon extra virgin olive oil

SERVES 4

spiced falafel burger

Falafels are Egyptian bean patties traditionally served in pita bread with salad leaves and hummus. Here they make a great burger filling with a tangy yogurt dressing. These burgers do need to be fried to prevent them becoming dry, but they can be finished for a minute or two on the grill to give them a slight smoky flavor before serving.

Put the dried chickpeas in a bowl and add cold water to cover by at least 5 inches. Let soak overnight. Drain the chickpeas well, transfer to a food processor, and blend until coarsely ground. Add the onion, garlic, parsley, cilantro, ground coriander, baking powder, and some salt and pepper and blend until very smooth. Transfer to a bowl, cover, and chill for 30 minutes.

To make the tahini sauce, put the yogurt, tahini, garlic, lemon juice, and olive oil in a bowl and whisk until smooth. Season to taste with salt and pepper and set aside until required.

Using wet hands, shape the chickpea mixture into 12 small or 8 medium patties. Heat a shallow layer of oil in a skillet, add the patties, and fry for 3 minutes on each side until golden and cooked through. Drain on paper towels.

Cut the rolls in half and fill with 2–3 patties, tahini yogurt sauce, salad leaves, and diced tomato. Serve hot.

6 ears of corn, husks removed

2 tablespoons extra virgin olive oil, plus extra to serve

3 ancho chile peppers

1½ tablespoons sea salt

3 limes, cut into wedges

SERVES 6

grilled corn
with chile-salt rub

One of the Southwest's most popular chiles is the ancho, the dried version of the poblano. When ground to a fine powder, it has a smoky flavor and is mild to medium on the heat scale—delicious with the sweet, nutty taste of corn.

Trim the ends of the corn. Bring a large saucepan of lightly salted water to a boil, add the corn, and boil for 5 minutes. Drain and refresh under cold water. Pat dry.

Preheat the grill until hot. Brush the corn with oil and cook on the grill for 6–8 minutes, turning frequently until charred all over.

Meanwhile, remove the stalk and seeds from the dried chiles. Chop the flesh coarsely and, using a spice grinder or mortar and pestle, grind to a fine powder. Transfer to a small bowl, then mix in the salt.

Rub the lime wedges vigorously over the corn, sprinkle with the chile salt, and serve with extra oil for drizzling.

chunky eggplant burgers
with pesto

1 large eggplant, about 1½ lb.

4 tablespoons extra virgin olive oil

1 tablespoon balsamic vinegar

1 garlic clove, crushed

4 soft bread rolls, halved

2 beefsteak tomatoes, thickly sliced

8 oz. mozzarella cheese, sliced

a handful of arugula leaves

sea salt and freshly ground black pepper

Pesto

1½ cups fresh basil leaves

1 garlic clove, crushed

4 tablespoons pine nuts

scant ½ cup extra virgin olive oil

2 tablespoons freshly grated Parmesan cheese

SERVES 4

The smoky taste of char-grilled eggplant and the basil pesto give these burgers a distinctive Mediterranean flavor. You could replace the fresh beefsteak tomatoes with semi-dried tomatoes if you like.

To make the pesto, put the basil, garlic, pine nuts, oil, and some salt and pepper in a food processor and blend until fairly smooth. Transfer to a bowl, stir in the Parmesan, and add more salt and pepper to taste. Set aside until required.

Cut the eggplant into ½-inch slices. Put the oil, vinegar, garlic, salt, and pepper in a bowl, whisk to mix, then brush over the eggplant slices. Cook them on a preheated hot grill for 3–4 minutes on each side until charred and softened.

Lightly toast the rolls and top with a slice of eggplant. Spread with pesto, add another slice of eggplant, then add a slice each of tomato and mozzarella. Drizzle with more pesto, then top with a few arugula leaves. Put the tops on the rolls and serve hot.

4 medium baking potatoes,

butter

sea salt and freshly ground
black pepper

SERVES 4

ember-roasted potatoes

**Roasting potatoes on the grill is so easy and the result
is a beautiful crispy skin and soft, fluffy insides. Just wrap
them in foil and leave them to sit in the embers while you
cook your meat and fish on the grill rack above.**

Wrap the potatoes individually in a double layer of foil and,
as soon as the coals are glowing red, put the potatoes on top.
Rake the charcoal up and around them, but without covering
them. Let cook for about 25 minutes, then, using tongs, turn
the potatoes over carefully and cook for a further 25–30 minutes
until cooked through.

Remove from the heat and carefully remove the foil, then cut
the potatoes in half. Serve, topped with a spoonful of butter,
salt, and pepper.

Variation

To cook sweet potatoes, follow the same method but cook for
about 20 minutes on each side.

Sweet potatoes are perfect for the grill because they cook quickly without pre-boiling. When tossed in dressing and wrapped in foil, the potatoes steam cook and absorb the flavors of the dressing. Care must be taken so that the potatoes do not burn through the foil where they are in direct contact with the heat. This recipe calls for individual packages, but one large package does just as well. Cook them before the meat and put them on one side of the grill to keep warm.

4 large sweet potatoes, about 1¼ lb., peeled and cut into 4 or 5 slices

1–2 tablespoons vegetable oil

1–2 tablespoons shoyu or tamari soy sauce

1 tablespoon sesame seeds

1 tablespoon finely chopped fresh parsley, to serve

a grill with a lid

SERVES 4

sesame sweet potato packages

Put the sweet potato in a bowl with the oil, soy sauce, and sesame seeds and toss well. Divide between 4 large squares of aluminum foil, then crinkle the foil up around them and close tightly. Put the foil packages on a preheated hot grill, close the lid, and let cook for 20–30 minutes or until tender. Alternatively, place the foil packages on a baking sheet and bake in a preheated oven at 350°F for 20 minutes or until tender.

When ready to serve, open up the packages and sprinkle a little parsley on the sweet potatoes.

Note An even easier way to cook sesame sweet potatoes is to boil the potatoes for 4–5 minutes or until tender, then drain and put in a bowl. Add the soy sauce, sesame seeds, and parsley and toss well.

Truly at home in both Middle Eastern and Mediterranean cuisines, eggplant is compatible with endless spices, herbs, and a multitude of other ingredients. In this dish, they soak up the fragrance of the spices and are perfectly paired with smoked cheese, enhancing the already smoky char-grilled flavor.

2 eggplant, cut lengthwise into about 5 slices

1 teaspoon chile oil

½ cup olive oil

3 teaspoons cumin seeds, lightly toasted in a dry skillet and ground

2 garlic cloves, crushed

1 red chile pepper, seeded and finely chopped

a large handful of fresh mint leaves, finely chopped

8 oz. firm smoked cheese, sliced

sea salt and freshly ground black pepper

a large handful of fresh cilantro, coarsely chopped, to serve

freshly squeezed juice of ½ lemon, to serve

MAKES 10 ROLLS

eggplant and smoked cheese rolls

Arrange the eggplant slices on a large tray. Mix the olive and chile oils, cumin, garlic, chile, mint, salt, and pepper in a measuring cup, then pour over the eggplant. Turn each slice over so that both sides are well coated. Cover with plastic wrap and set aside for a few hours or overnight to soak up all the flavors.

Put the eggplant on a preheated grill or smoking-hot stove-top grill pan. Cook for about 4 minutes, then turn and cook the other side until tender and browned.

Remove from the heat, put some of the cheese at one end of a slice of eggplant, and roll up firmly (do this while the eggplant is still hot so the cheese melts). Repeat with the other slices. Sprinkle with the cilantro and lemon juice, then serve.

10 oz. firm tofu, rinsed, drained, patted dry, and cut into bite-sized cubes

leaves from a small bunch of fresh basil, shredded

sesame oil, for frying

Marinade

3 lemongrass stalks, trimmed and finely chopped

1 tablespoon peanut oil

3 tablespoons soy sauce

1–2 fresh red chile peppers, seeded and finely chopped

2 garlic cloves, crushed

1 teaspoon ground turmeric

2 teaspoons sugar

sea salt

Soy dipping sauce

4–5 tablespoons soy sauce

1–2 tablespoons Thai fish sauce

freshly squeezed juice of 1 lime

1–2 teaspoons sugar

1 fresh red chile pepper, seeded and finely chopped

a packet of wooden or bamboo skewers, soaked in water before use

SERVES 3–4

spicy tofu satay
with soy dipping sauce

Here is a very tasty dish that does wonderful things to tofu, which can be rather bland. Full of the flavors of Southeast Asia, this tasty Vietnamese snack is perfect as an appetizer or as part of a vegetarian selection at a cook-out, but is sure to be enjoyed by all!

To make the marinade, mix the lemongrass, peanut oil, soy sauce, chile, garlic, and turmeric with the sugar until it has dissolved. Add a little salt to taste and toss in the tofu, making sure it is well coated. Leave to marinate for 1 hour.

Prepare the soy dipping sauce by whisking all the ingredients together. Set aside until ready to serve.

Preheat the grill. Thread the tofu cubes onto the skewers and grill them for 2–3 minutes on each side. Serve the tofu hot, garnished with the shredded basil and with the dipping sauce on the side.

plantain *with lime and chile*

2 plantains, thinly sliced diagonally

freshly squeezed juice of 1 lime

1 tablespoon chile oil

sea salt

fresh cilantro, coarsely chopped, to serve

SERVES 4

Plantain lends itself very well to grills. The cooking process brings out its sweetness, so it's good to offset that with a bit of citrus and chile. Plantain is readily available from some supermarkets or speciality Caribbean shops.

Put the slices of plantain in a large bowl with the lime juice and chile oil. Carefully turn them over to cover evenly (this will stop them discoloring).

Arrange the slices on a preheated grill or stove-top grill pan and cook for 2–3 minutes or until slightly charred. Gently turn them over, using a palette knife, then cook the other side for 2 minutes. (The plantain changes from a fleshy color to a beautiful bright yellow blackened with the stripes of the grill.)

When cooked, lift onto a plate, sprinkle with salt and fresh cilantro, then serve.

Note When plantains are ripe and at their best for cooking, they have blackened skins and look like ordinary bananas that have gone past their best.

salads & sides

mayonnaise

Mayonnaise is the perfect accompaniment to grilled foods, and homemade is all the better. When making it, try to use a regular olive oil rather than extra virgin, which can make the sauce bitter.

2 egg yolks

2 teaspoons white wine vinegar or lemon juice

2 teaspoons Dijon mustard

¼ teaspoon salt

1¼ cups olive oil

freshly ground black pepper

MAKES ABOUT 1¼ CUPS

Put the egg yolks, vinegar, mustard, and salt into a food processor and blend briefly until frothy. With the machine running, gradually pour in the olive oil in a slow steady stream until all the oil is incorporated and the sauce is thick and glossy.

If the sauce is too thick, add 1–2 tablespoons boiling water and blend again briefly. Season to taste with salt and pepper, then cover the surface of the mayonnaise with plastic wrap. Store in the refrigerator for up to 3 days.

creamy coleslaw

No grill would be complete without a classic coleslaw on the side. This one uses homemade mayonnaise, but if you are short on time you can always substitute with a store-bought brand.

8 oz. white cabbage, thinly sliced

6 oz. carrots, grated, about 1½ cups

½ white onion, thinly sliced

1 teaspoon salt

2 teaspoons sugar

1 tablespoon white wine vinegar

¼ cup Mayonnaise (left)

2 tablespoons heavy cream

1 tablespoon whole-grain mustard

sea salt and freshly ground black pepper

SERVES 4

Put the white cabbage, carrots, and onion into a colander and sprinkle with the salt, sugar, and vinegar. Stir well and let drain over a bowl for 30 minutes.

Squeeze out excess liquid from the vegetables and put into a large bowl. Put the mayonnaise, cream, and mustard into a separate bowl and mix well, then stir into the cabbage mixture. Season to taste with salt and pepper and serve. Store in the refrigerator for up to 3 days.

This satisfying summer salad with a delicious hint of fresh mint makes a superb accompaniment to grilled meat or fish. It also makes a great vegetarian option.

zucchini, feta, and mint salad

1 tablespoon sesame seeds

6 large zucchini

3 tablespoons extra virgin olive oil

6 oz. feta cheese, crumbled

a handful of fresh mint leaves

Dressing

4 tablespoons extra virgin olive oil

1 tablespoon lemon juice

1 small garlic clove, crushed

sea salt and freshly ground black pepper

SERVES 4

Put the sesame seeds into a dry skillet and toast over medium heat until golden and aromatic. Remove from the heat, let cool, and set aside until required.

Preheat the grill. Cut the zucchini diagonally into thick slices, toss with the olive oil, and season with salt and pepper. Cook over hot coals for 2–3 minutes on each side until charred and tender. Remove and let cool.

Put all the dressing ingredients into a screw-top jar and shake well. Add salt and pepper to taste.

Put the zucchini, feta, and mint into a large bowl, add the dressing, and toss well until evenly coated. Sprinkle with the sesame seeds and serve at once.

Vegetables taste wonderful when cooked on the grill—it brings out their natural sweetness. Look out for the long, cubanelle peppers in farmers' markets—they are especially good grilled. This salad serves four as an entrée or six as an appetizer.

salad of roasted bell pepper and asparagus

½ red onion, sliced

6 red bell peppers

1 lb. asparagus spears, trimmed

extra virgin olive oil, for brushing

8 oz. snowpeas

4 oz. mixed salad leaves

a handful of fresh parsley and dill leaves

2 oz. hazelnuts, about ¾ cup, toasted and coarsely chopped

Hazelnut oil dressing

4 tablespoons hazelnut oil

2 tablespoons extra virgin olive oil

1 tablespoon sherry vinegar

1 teaspoon sugar

sea salt and freshly ground black pepper

SERVES 4–6

Put the sliced onion into a strainer, sprinkle with salt, and let drain over a bowl for 30 minutes. Rinse under cold running water and pat dry with paper towels.

Preheat the grill, then cook the bell peppers over hot coals for 15 minutes, turning frequently until charred all over. Transfer to a plastic bag, seal, and let soften until cool. Peel off the skin and discard the seeds, then cut the flesh into thick strips.

Brush the asparagus with olive oil and cook over hot coals for 3–4 minutes, turning frequently, until charred and tender.

Put the snowpeas into a large saucepan of lightly salted boiling water and boil for 1–2 minutes. Drain and refresh under cold running water.

Put the onion, peppers, asparagus, and mangetout into a large bowl and toss gently. Add the salad leaves, herbs, and hazelnuts. Put the dressing ingredients into a bowl and whisk well, then pour over the salad and toss until coated. Serve.

8 oz. fresh mozzarella cheese, drained

1 large green bell pepper, seeded and chopped

1 Lebanese (mini) cucumber, chopped

2 ripe tomatoes, chopped

½ red onion, finely chopped

2 pita breads

4 tablespoons extra virgin olive oil

freshly squeezed juice of ½ lemon

sea salt and freshly ground black pepper

Olive salsa

3 oz. Kalamata olives, pitted and chopped

1 tablespoon chopped fresh parsley

1 small garlic clove, finely chopped

4 tablespoons extra virgin olive oil

1 tablespoon freshly squeezed lemon juice

freshly ground black pepper

SERVES 4

grilled pita salad
with olive salsa and mozzarella

Fatoush is a bread salad made from grilled pita bread. It's often accompanied by haloumi, a firm cheese that can be char-grilled. This recipe uses fresh mozzarella cheese, which can also be cooked on the grill and picks up an appealing smokiness in the process.

Wrap the mozzarella in paper towels and squeeze gently to remove excess water. Unwrap and cut into thick slices. Brush the slices well with olive oil and place them on the grill. Cook over the hot coals for 1 minute on each side until the cheese is charred with lines and beginning to soften. Alternatively, simply slice the cheese and use without grilling.

Put the green bell pepper, cucumber, tomatoes, and onion into a bowl. Toast the pita breads over hot coals, cool slightly, then tear into bite-sized pieces. Add to the bowl, then pour over the olive oil and lemon juice. Season and stir well.

Put all the ingredients for the olive salsa into a bowl and stir well.

Spoon the salad onto small plates, top with a few slices of mozzarella and some olive salsa, then serve.

tabbouleh *with chickpeas and spring salad*

½ cup fine bulgur (cracked wheat)

2 tablespoons freshly squeezed lemon juice

¼ cup extra virgin olive oil

1 small basket of cherry tomatoes, halved

1 large handful of fresh mint leaves, finely chopped

2 tablespoons finely chopped dill

1 small bunch of fresh flatleaf parsley, finely chopped

14 oz. can chickpeas, rinsed and drained

4–5 oz. spring salad mix

sea salt and freshly ground black pepper

toasted Turkish flat bread, to serve

SERVES 4

It's fun to hand-pick salad leaves, making up your own mix. You will find big barrels or bags of lovely tender spring salad greens at your local market. When buying greens, keep in mind you will need about two large handfuls per person. Avoid limp looking greens. If they do wilt a little on the way home on warmer days, give them a quick bath in a bowl of cold water with a pinch or two of sugar thrown in. This will freshen them up. The spring fresh ingredients are combined here with bulgur. Simply cover with boiling water to soften and add to your favorite salad ingredients.

Put the bulgur in a heatproof bowl and pour over ½ cup boiling water. Stir once, cover tightly with plastic wrap, and set aside for 8–10 minutes. Put the lemon juice and olive oil in a small bowl and whisk. Pour over the bulgur and stir well with a fork, fluffing up the bulgur and separating the grains.

Put the bulgur in a large bowl with the tomatoes, mint, dill, parsley, chickpeas, and salad greens. Use your hands to toss everything together. Season well with salt and pepper. Transfer to a serving plate and serve with toasted Turkish flat bread.

Tabbouleh, the fresh parsley salad from Lebanon, is based on bulgur wheat. This one is made with couscous, the fine Moroccan pasta, available in an instant version—you just soak it in water or stock for 10 minutes or so. It makes a quick and easy side for grilled foods and the grains soak up the lovely meat or fish juices and add flavor.

1½ cups instant couscous

freshly squeezed juice of 1 lemon

2 tablespoons chopped fresh basil

2 tablespoons chopped fresh cilantro

2 tablespoons chopped fresh mint

2 tablespoons chopped fresh parsley

sea salt and freshly ground black pepper

2 lemons, halved, to serve

Fragrant garlic oil

1 whole head of garlic, cloves separated

2 bay leaves

2¾ cups extra virgin olive oil

SERVES 4

fragrant herb couscous salad

To make the fragrant garlic oil, peel the cloves and put them into a saucepan. Add the bay leaves and oil and heat gently for 15 minutes until the garlic has softened. Don't let the garlic brown. Let cool, remove and mash the garlic cloves, then return them to the oil. Refrigerate until required. Use 1¼ cups for this recipe and reserve the remainder.

Put the couscous into a bowl, add boiling water to cover by 2 inches, and let soak for 10 minutes.

Drain the soaked couscous, shaking the strainer well to remove any excess water. Transfer to a bowl, add the fragrant garlic oil, lemon juice, chopped basil, cilantro, mint, and parsley. Season with salt and pepper, then set aside to develop the flavors until ready to serve. Serve with halved lemons.

2 teaspoons sea salt

7 oz. instant polenta, about 1⅓ cups

2 garlic cloves, crushed

1 tablespoon chopped fresh basil

4 tablespoons butter

2 oz. freshly grated Parmesan cheese, about ½ cup

freshly ground black pepper

olive oil, for brushing

a rectangular cake pan, 9 x 12 inches, greased

SERVES 8

grilled polenta

Grilled polenta triangles make a lovely accompaniment for grilled meats and fish or they can be used as a bruschetta-type base for grilled vegetables.

Pour 1 quart water into a heavy-based saucepan and bring to a boil. Add the salt and gradually whisk in the polenta in a steady stream, using a large, metal whisk.

Cook over low heat, stirring constantly with a wooden spoon, for 5 minutes or until the grains have swelled and thickened.

Remove the saucepan from the heat and immediately beat in the garlic, basil, butter, and Parmesan until the mixture is smooth. Season to taste with black pepper. Pour into the greased tin and let cool completely.

Preheat the grill. Turn out the polenta onto a board and cut into large squares, then cut in half again to form triangles. Brush the triangles with a little olive oil and cook over hot coals for 2–3 minutes on each side until charred and heated through.

chile cornbread

½ cup all-purpose flour

1 tablespoon baking powder

1⅓ cups medium cornmeal
or polenta

1 teaspoon salt

3 eggs, beaten

1¼ cups buttermilk

4 tablespoons extra virgin olive oil

8 oz. canned corn kernels, about
1 cup, drained

1–2 red chile peppers, seeded
and chopped

2 tablespoons chopped
fresh cilantro

*a deep loaf pan, 2 lb., greased
and bottom-lined with parchment
paper*

SERVES 8–12

This flavorsome cornbread is great served in big chunks
to mop up the delicious juices of grilled meat, fish, or
vegetables. It is handy to cook it in a deep loaf pan so that
later it can be sliced and toasted more easily. However, if
you are short of time, pour the mixture into a greased and
base-lined baking pan and cook for 20–25 minutes.

Preheat the oven to 400°F.

Sift the flour and baking powder into a bowl and stir in the
cornmeal and salt.

Mix the eggs, buttermilk, and oil in a second bowl, then, using
a wooden spoon, stir into the dry ingredients to make a smooth
batter. Stir in the corn, chile, and cilantro and pour into the
prepared loaf pan.

Bake in the preheated oven for 40 minutes. Let cool in the pan for
5 minutes, then remove from the tin and let cool on a wire rack.

grilled rosemary flatbread

1⅔ cups bread flour, plus extra for dusting

1½ teaspoons active dry yeast

1 teaspoon salt

1 tablespoon chopped fresh rosemary

2 tablespoons extra virgin olive oil, plus extra for brushing

SERVES 4

Hot from the grill, this aromatic herb bread is delicious used to mop up any wonderful meat juices, or eaten on its own with olive oil for dipping.

Sift the flour into the bowl of an electric mixer and stir in the yeast, salt, and rosemary. Add ½ cup of hot water and the olive oil and knead with the dough hook at high speed for about 8 minutes or until the dough is smooth and elastic.

Alternatively, sift the flour into a large bowl and stir in the yeast, salt, and rosemary. Make a well in the centre, then add the hot water and olive oil and mix to form a soft dough. Turn out onto a lightly floured work surface and knead until the dough is smooth and elastic.

Shape the dough into a ball, then put into an oiled bowl, cover with a dish towel, and let rise in a warm place for 45–60 minutes or until doubled in size.

Punch down the dough and divide into quarters. Roll each piece out on a lightly floured work surface to make a 6-inches long oval.

Preheat the grill to a low heat. Brush the bread with a little olive oil and cook for 5 minutes, then brush the top with the remaining olive oil, flip, and cook for a further 4–5 minutes until the bread is cooked through. Serve hot.

garlic bread skewers

This is a fun version of garlic bread, and the slightly smoky flavor you get from the coals is delicious. You can also add cubes of cheese such as mozzarella or Fontina to the skewers.

1 baguette

⅔ cup extra virgin olive oil

2 garlic cloves, crushed

2 tablespoons chopped fresh parsley

sea salt and freshly ground black pepper

6–8 wooden or bamboo skewers, soaked in water before use.

SERVES 6–8

Cut the bread into 1-inch thick slices, then cut the slices crosswise to make half moons.

Put the olive oil, garlic, parsley, salt, and pepper into a large bowl, add the bread, and toss until well coated with the parsley and oil.

Preheat the grill. Thread the garlic bread onto skewers and cook over medium hot coals for 2–3 minutes on each side until toasted.

Variation

Cut 8 oz. mozzarella cheese into about 24 small pieces. Thread a piece of bread onto the skewer and continue to alternate the cheese and bread. Cook as in the main recipe.

sweet things

Wrapping fruits in foil is a great way to cook them on the grill—all the juices are contained in the package while the fruit softens.

grilled fruit packages

4 peaches or nectarines, halved, pitted, and sliced

8 oz. blueberries, 1½ cups

4 oz. raspberries, ¾ cup

freshly squeezed juice of 1 orange

1 teaspoon ground cinnamon

2 tablespoons sugar

1 cup thick yogurt

2 tablespoons heavy cream

1 tablespoon clear honey

1 tablespoon rose water

1 tablespoon chopped pistachio nuts, to serve

SERVES 4

Put the fruit into a large bowl, add the orange juice, cinnamon, and sugar and mix well. Divide the fruit mixture evenly between 4 sheets of foil. Fold the foil over the fruit and seal the edges to make packages.

Put the yogurt, honey, and rosewater into a separate bowl and mix well. Set aside until required.

Preheat the grill, then cook the packages over medium hot coals for 5–6 minutes. Remove the packages from the heat, open carefully, and transfer to 4 serving bowls. Serve with the yogurt and a sprinkling of pistachio nuts.

grilled figs *with almond*

mascarpone cream

This dish works well with stone fruits too, such as plums, peaches or nectarines.

6 oz. mascarpone cheese

½ teaspoon vanilla extract

1 tablespoon toasted
ground almonds, or slivered
almonds crushed to a powder
with a mortar and pestle

1 tablespoon Marsala wine

1 tablespoon clear honey

1 tablespoon sugar

1 teaspoon ground cardamom

8–10 figs, halved

SERVES 4

Put the mascarpone cheese, vanilla extract, almonds, Marsala wine, and honey into a bowl and beat well. Set aside in the refrigerator until required.

Put the sugar and ground cardamom into a separate bowl and mix well. Carefully dip the cut surface of the figs into the mixture.

Preheat the grill, then cook the figs over medium hot coals for 1–2 minutes on each side until charred and softened.

Transfer the grilled figs to 4 serving bowls and serve with the almond mascarpone cream.

banana packages
with chocolate and rum

4 banana leaves or aluminum foil, cut to 10 inches square

4 bananas, halved crosswise

4 oz. dark chocolate, broken into small pieces

4 tablespoons dark rum

1 tablespoon safflower oil (if using a grill pan)

whipped cream, to serve

kitchen twine or raffia, soaked in water for 15 minutes before use

SERVES 4

Ever so slightly decadent, this dish will help you re-create the taste of the Caribbean in minutes. Equally good cooked outside on a grill in the heat of summer or made on a stove-top grill pan in the depths of winter.

Put the banana leaves on a work surface. On the first leaf, put 2 banana halves side by side. Sprinkle with one-quarter of the chocolate and 1 tablespoon rum. Fold up the sides and edges to form a square parcel. Tie with the wet string or raffia (soaking will prevent the string from burning). Repeat to make 4 packages.

Put the packages on a preheated grill or oiled, smoking-hot stove-top grill pan and cook for about 10 minutes on each side.

Snip the twine and serve with whipped cream.

Note Banana leaves are available from Latin-American markets or Asian stores. To make them more malleable, put on the grill or grill pan for 1 minute before using. Aluminum foil makes a worthy substitute.

A simple but delicious end to a meal—the pears, blue cheese, and walnuts perfectly complement one another. Serve on toast with a glass or two of dessert wine. For the best results, choose ripe but firm pears.

grilled pears with spiced honey, walnuts, and blue cheese

2 oz. walnuts

2 tablespoons clear honey

¼ teaspoon ground cardamom

4 pears

2 tablespoons sugar, for dusting

4 slices of toast

4 oz. Gorgonzola cheese

dessert wine, to serve

SERVES 4

Put the walnuts into a skillet, add the honey and cardamom, and cook over a high heat until the honey bubbles furiously and starts to darken. Immediately pour the mixture onto a sheet of waxed paper and let cool.

Peel the nuts from the paper and set aside.

Preheat the grill. Using a sharp knife, cut the pears into quarters and remove and discard the cores. Cut the pear quarters into thick wedges. Dust lightly with sugar and cook over medium hot coals for about 1½ minutes on each side.

Pile the pears onto slices of toast, sprinkle with the walnuts, and crumble over some Gorgonzola cheese. Serve with a glass of dessert wine.

s'mores

16 cookies

8 pieces of plain chocolate

16 marshmallows

8 metal skewers

SERVES 4

This is one for the kids. S'mores are a campfire classic: grilled marshmallows and chocolate squares sandwiched together in a delicious, gooey taste sensation. Sweet biscuits, such as langue du chat or almond thins, work just as well as graham crackers, but any will do.

Put half the cookies onto a plate and top each one with a square of chocolate.

Preheat the grill. Thread 2 marshmallows onto each skewer and cook over hot coals for about 2 minutes, turning constantly until the marshmallows are melted and blackened. Remove from the heat and let cool slightly.

Put the marshmallows onto the chocolate squares and sandwich together with the remaining cookies. Gently ease out the skewers and serve the s'mores as soon as the chocolate melts.

thinly pared peel and freshly squeezed juice of 6 large unwaxed lemons

¾ cup sugar

sparkling water, to top up

To serve

ice cubes

fresh lemon slices

sprigs of fresh mint

SERVES 6–8

homemade fresh lemonade

Fresh lemonade is simple to make and you can keep the lemony syrup in the fridge and dilute it with either chilled sparkling water or soda water as required. You could also try adding saffron to make a golden-hued drink with an intriguing taste. Just add a pinch of saffron threads to the warm syrup when you take it off the heat.

Put the lemon zest, sugar, and 2½ cups of water in a saucepan and bring slowly to a simmer, stirring to dissolve the sugar. As soon as the sugar is dissolved and the syrup begins to bubble, take it off the heat. Half-cover and leave until cold.

Squeeze the lemons and add the juice to the cold syrup. Strain into a bowl, cover, and chill.

Transfer the lemonade to a glass pitcher filled with ice cubes and add the lemon slices and mint. Dilute with sparkling water on a ratio of about 1 part syrup to 1 part water.

2 fresh peaches, pitted and thinly sliced

9 oz. strawberries, hulled and sliced

1 orange, sliced

⅔ cup crème de fraise (strawberry-flavored liqueur)

2 x 750-ml bottles (6 cups) dry white wine

1 small cucumber, peeled, seeded, and thinly sliced

clear sparkling lemonade, to top up

borage flowers (optional), to serve

ice cubes, to serve

SERVES 12

peach and strawberry sangria

This is a fragrant and more delicate version of the classic Spanish sangria. You can add almost any fruit you like and vary the liqueur to your taste. Try peach schnapps or crème de framboise (raspberry-flavored liqueur).

Put the peaches, strawberries, and orange slices in a large pitcher with the strawberry liqueur. Pour in the wine and chill for 30 minutes. When ready to serve, add the cucumber and some ice and top up with lemonade. Pour into glasses and garnish each serving with borage flowers, if using.

cosmopolitan iced tea

1 oz. vodka, vanilla-flavored if available

½ oz. triple sec

⅓ cup cranberry juice

freshly squeezed juice of ½ lime

ice cubes

SERVES 1

Cranberry juice lends a light, fruity, refreshing quality to this cocktail, where it's natural bitterness is softened by the triple sec.

Fill a cocktail shaker with ice. Add the vodka, triple sec, and cranberry and lime juices. Replace the lid and shake briskly. Strain into a tall glass, half-filled with ice. Serve immediately.

index

conversion charts

Weights and measures have been rounded up or down slightly to make measuring easier.

Volume equivalents:

American	Metric	Imperial
1 teaspoon	5 ml	
1 tablespoon	15 ml	
¼ cup	60 ml	2 fl.oz.
⅓ cup	75 ml	2½ fl.oz.
½ cup	125 ml	4 fl.oz.
⅔ cup	150 ml	5 fl.oz. (¼ pint)
¾ cup	175 ml	6 fl.oz.
1 cup	250 ml	8 fl.oz.

1 stick butter = 8 tablespoons = 125 g

Weight equivalents:

Imperial	Metric
1 oz.	25 g
2 oz.	50 g
3 oz.	75 g
4 oz.	125 g
5 oz.	150 g
6 oz.	175 g
7 oz.	200 g
8 oz. (½ lb.)	250 g
9 oz.	275 g
10 oz.	300 g
11 oz.	325 g
12 oz.	375 g
13 oz.	400 g
14 oz.	425 g
15 oz.	475 g
16 oz. (1 lb.)	500 g
2 lb.	1 kg

Measurements:

Inches	Cm
¼ inch	5 mm
½ inch	1 cm
¾ inch	1.5 cm
1 inch	2.5 cm
2 inches	5 cm
3 inches	7 cm
4 inches	10 cm
5 inches	12 cm
6 inches	15 cm
7 inches	18 cm
8 inches	20 cm
9 inches	23 cm
10 inches	25 cm
11 inches	28 cm
12 inches	30 cm

Oven temperatures:

110°C	(225°F)	Gas ¼
120°C	(250°F)	Gas ½
140°C	(275°F)	Gas 1
150°C	(300°F)	Gas 2
160°C	(325°F)	Gas 3
180°C	(350°F)	Gas 4
190°C	(375°F)	Gas 5
200°C	(400°F)	Gas 6
220°C	(425°F)	Gas 7
230°C	(450°F)	Gas 8
240°C	(475°F)	Gas 9

recipe credits

Ghillie Başan
char-grilled tamarind
  shrimp
chicken tandoori
  kabobs
cumin-flavored lamb
  kabobs with hot
  hummus
curried pork satay with
  pineapple sauce
duck satay with grilled
  pineapple and plum
  sauce
fiery beef satay in
  peanut sauce
harissa chicken kabobs
  with oranges and
  preserved lemon
lamb and porcini
  kabobs with sage
  and Parmesan
lamb shish kabob
  with yogurt and
  flatbread
monkfish kabobs with
  chermoula
pork kofta kabobs with
  sweet and sour
  sauce
shrimp and scallop
  kabobs with walnut
  sauce
spicy beef and coconut
  kofta kabobs
spicy chicken kabobs
  with ground almonds
spicy tofu satay with
  soy dipping sauce
stuffed char-grilled
  sardines
summer vegetable
  kabobs with
  homemade pesto
swordfish kabobs with
  oranges and sumac
vine-wrapped fish
  kabobs with tangy
  herb sauce

Fiona Beckett
Argentinian-style
  "asado" steak with
  chimichurri salsa
char-grilled steak fajitas
  with chunky
  guacamole
corn and pepper salsa
fresh tomato salsa
salsa verde

Sicilian-spiced sea
  bass with grilled
  tomatoes and baby
  fennel
Tuscan-style steak

Maxine Clark
grilled salmon steaks
  with basil and
  Parmesan butter
mustard-grilled salmon
  tail

Ross Dobson
summer tabbouleh with
  chickpeas and spring
  salad

Jane Noraika
banana packages with
  chocolate and rum
eggplant and smoked
  cheese rolls
plantain with lime and
  chile

**Elsa Petersen-
Schepelern**
baba ganoush
barbecued spareribs
  with Mexican salsa
char-grilled shrimp with
  avocado chile salsa

Louise Pickford
Asian barbecue sauce
barbecue sauce
barbecued fish bathed
  in oregano and
  lemon
barbecued Mexican-
  style Cornish hens
grilled pears with spiced
  honey, walnuts, and
  blue cheese
beet and pearl onion
  brochettes
butterflied lamb with
  white bean salad
caper butter
cheeseburger
chicken lemon
  skewers
chicken kabobs
  Moroccan-style
chicken "panini" with
  mozzarella and salsa
  rossa
chicken steak burger

with Caesar dressing
chile cornbread
chile jam
chunky eggplant
  burgers with pesto
clam packages with
  garlic butter
cosmopolitan ice tea
creamy coleslaw
creamy corn salsa
Creole rub
duck yakitori
dukkah crusted tuna
  with preserved lemon
  salsa
ember-roasted
  potatoes
fragrant Asian rub
fragrant herb couscous
  salad
garlic bread skewers
grilled corn with
  chile-salt rub
grilled figs with almond
  mascarpone cream
grilled fruit packages
grilled pita salad with
  olive salsa and
  mozzarella
grilled polenta
grilled rosemary
  flatbread
grilling basics text
homemade fresh
  lemonade
herb butter
herb, lemon, and garlic
  marinade
hot pineapple and
  papaya salsa
jerk chicken wings with
  avocado salsa
lamb burgers with mint
  yogurt
mayonnaise
minted yogurt
  marinade
Moroccan fish skewers
  with couscous
Moroccan rub
mushroom burgers with
  caramelized garlic
  aïoli
olive-infused chicken
  with charred lemons
open chicken burger
  with grilled
  vegetables
open Tex-Mex burger
  with chile relish
parsley, feta, and pine
  nut dip
peach and strawberry
  sangria

peppered tuna steak
  with salsa rossa
piri-piri sauce
red snapper with
  parsley salad
red bell pepper butter
  sauce
sage-rubbed pork
  chops
saffron butter
salad of roasted bell
  peppers and
  asparagus
"sausage" burgers for
  kids
seared swordfish with
  new potatoes,
  beans, and olives
shrimp with chile oil
  and pistachio and
  mint pesto
skewered scallops with
  coconut dressing
smoky barbecue sauce
s'mores
souvlaki with cracked
  wheat salad
spiced falafel burger
spiced pork burger with
  satay sauce
squid piri-piri
steak with blue cheese
  butter
sweet chile sauce
Tex-Mex pork rack
Thai spice marinade
tomato, sesame, and
  ginger salsa
top dogs
Vietnamese pork
  balls
whole chicken roasted
  on the grill
whole salmon stuffed
  with herbs
zucchini, feta, and mint
  salad

Fiona Smith
guacamole
roast garlic, paprika,
  and sherry alioli
roast tomato ketchup
sweet chile and tomato
  salsa
tomato, lemon, and
  zucchini relish
tzatziki

Lindy Wildsmith
aromatic pork burger in
  pitta bread
char-grilled chicken
  breast with mixed

leaves and balsamic
  dressing
chile tomato chutney
grilling basics text
mango, kiwi, and
  cilantro salsa

parsley and anchovy
  relish
peperonata
sesame sweet potato
  packets

picture credits

Key: *a*=above, *b*=below, *r*=right, *l*=left, *c*=center,
bg= background.

Martin Brigdale
Pages 4–5, 6, 9*al*, 10*bl*,
18, 37, 48, 50 inset, 51,
52, 59, 60, 64, 80, 83,
98, 101, 110, 129, 131,
163, 177, 181, 185,
188, 189, 219

Peter Cassidy
Pages 23, 27 inset, 29,
85, 90 inset, 92, 109,
117, 137, 140, 149,
155, 162, 165, 180,
208 inset, 209, 212
inset, 213, 215 inset,
221

Christopher Drake
Page 10*cl*

Daniel Farmer
Page 108

Richard Jung
Pages 3, 35, 44, 54–56,
66, 72–76, 87, 88, 96,
104*bg*, 112, 114–116,
118, 121, 125, 132
inset, 145–147, 154,
157, 161, 164, 166,
172, 174, 179, 184,
193, 195, 196, 206,
215*bg*, 230 inset, 231,
234 inset

Lisa Linder
Page 233

William Lingwood
Pages 31 inset, 138,
141, 190, 194, 224,
232, 235

Diana Miller
Pages 30, 33, 38, 39
inset, 41, 45, 136, 152,
225

David Munns
Pages 62 inset, 200

William Reavell
Pages 216, 226

Debi Treloar
Pages 7, 13, 47, 58
inset, 69, 78 inset, 104
inset, 187 inset, 191
inset

Ian Wallace
Pages 1, 2, 8, 9 *ac, ar*
& *b*, 10 *al, ar,* & *br,* 11,
12, 14, 17, 19, 21, 22,
25, 26, 34, 42, 46, 63,
67, 68, 71, 79, 84, 91,
95, 97, 102, 105–107,
113, 122, 126, 128,
130, 133, 134, 139,
142, 143 inset, 150,
153, 158, 159 inset,
160, 169–171, 173,
178, 182, 183, 186,
197, 198, 201–203,
205, 210, 211, 214,
217, 218, 220, 222,
223, 227, 228

Kate Whitaker
Pages 16, 20, 24,
27*bg*, 31*bg*, 39*bg*, 40,
43, 50*bg*, 58*bg*, 62*bg*,
70, 78*bg*, 82, 89, 90*bg*,
94, 100, 111, 119, 123,
124, 132*bg*, 135,
143*bg*, 151, 159*bg*,
168, 175, 176, 187*bg*,
191*bg*, 192, 199, 204,
208*bg*, 212*bg*, 229*bg*,
230*bg*, 234*bg*

Polly Wreford
Page 229 inset